Mindful

How to Overcome Mental Strongholds
& Change Your Life For Good

Do you ever doubt the promises of God? Are you constantly rehearsing your own negative thoughts? Do you feel like you're never truly at peace with yourself? Pastor Matthew Ochoa's new book, "Mindful" will reveal to you the root of these issues in a simple, but profound way. Giving you a play-by-play game plan of how you can win the battle that's in your mind. Pastor Ochoa is gifted by the Lord to communicate Biblical truth that will set you free and enable you to change your life for good! I can wholeheartedly recommend "Mindful" without reservation, and I am honored to be associated with Pastor Ochoa.

Ashley Terradez
Founder and President, Terradez Ministries,
Global Church Family and Power Academy
www.terradez.com

Pastor Matthew is not only a pastor and an excellent teacher, but he is also my friend. The first time I read one of his books, I thought, "I like this guy." In this book, Pastor Matthew teaches about God's character and His will for your life. Not only that, but you'll learn how to hold onto God's words for your life so that you can see them come to reality.

Dustin Barker
Founder of Dustin Barker Ministries
Christian Author and Speaker
www.dbministries.com

Our success in this life is determined by the mentalities we build, maintain and occupy. In Mindful, Pastor Matthew sheds light on mentalities that need to be built and those that need to be destroyed so that you can change your life for the good. You can overcome mental strongholds and enjoy the life God has for you!

Kerrick Butler II
Senior Pastor of Faith Christian Center
www.kerrickbutler.com

In Colossians 3:2, the Apostle Paul tells us to "set our minds on things above, not on earthly things." My friend Matthew helps you do that in this book. In a world caught up on earthly things, this book provides insights and concepts to help you become mindful of the things above. So grab some fresh chicken and dumplings and get ready to receive practical life-changing wisdom from the word of God.

Elijah Murrell
Founder of Murrell Ministries International
www.murrellministries.com

Mindful

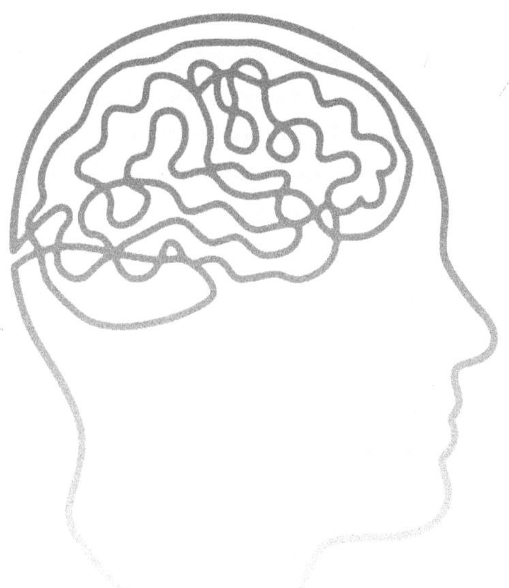

How to Overcome Mental Strongholds
& Change Your Life For Good

Matthew Ochoa

Mindful: How to Overcome Mental Strongholds & Changing Your Life For Good
ISBN 979-8-3304-4922-4

Published in partnership by Deep Rooted Ministries and Matthew Ochoa Ministries

www.matthewochoa.com | www.deeprooted.church

Stephanie,
your love, support, and encouragement are what keep me going. I would not know how to do what I do without you.

You are a great wife, mother, homemaker, and pastor. I knew you were the one from the moment I met you, and I'm proud to admit I was right.

I love you.

Matthew and my new son (who is not yet named at the time of writing this),
I love being called your dad.

I can't wait to see what God has in store for the both of you. I don't know what it will be, but I know it will be filled with wonder and adventure.

I love you both so much. May God's will be evident in your lives always.

Deep Rooted,
since I was in high school, I had visions of what a healthy, grounded, and loving church would look like.

At the time, I had no idea how it would happen or when.

Thank you for making a difference in the lives of our community and all over the world.

The Apostle Paul would be so proud of this church. Jesus is proud of this church.

CONTENTS

Foreword

Mindful is a masterclass in renewing your mind. If you're looking for a book that goes beyond surface level advice and delves into the heart of true transformation, this is it! There are so many truths in this book that can help you make little adjustments in your life that can change everything!

It's like a roadmap on how to navigate in a social climate that receives almost everything that is thrown at them without question, and in many cases accepts it as part of them. Matthew shows you line upon line how you can actually change your thinking, and expertly walks you through how to apply this wisdom in your daily life. His approach is both refreshing and empowering!

He takes an area that once was dark and hard to see and shines a light on it-the light of the Word of God. One of the most important things you can learn in this life is what to resist and what to yield to, and Matthew shows you how to walk that out in everyday life. He shows you how small shifts in your thinking can lead to major breakthroughs in your life. This book isn't just another book on mind renewal, it's a manual for a transformed life. Having read many books on the subject over the past few decades, I can confidently say this one stands at the top! I highly recommend it.

Pastor RayGene Wilson
Lead Pastor and Founder, West Coast Life Church, Murrieta, CA
Internationally Known Gospel Singer and Recording Artist
Author of *Faith Has A Voice*
www.westcoastlife.tv

Introduction

Have you ever wondered why some people seem to live victorious lives while others struggle daily? What if I told you that the difference lies in one simple yet profound truth: the power of their mind? Your mind is the most powerful tool you have access to. This book isn't about mind control and how to manipulate people; it's about learning how to use your mind to your benefit through the foundational truths found in God's Word.

In the book of Proverbs, it says, "For as he thinks in his heart, so is he" (Proverbs 23:7). This statement reveals that your life is going in the direction of your most dominant thoughts. Your current circumstances and how your life unfolds are directly influenced by how you think. You can experience a victorious life or a defeated life simply based on how your thoughts are programmed.

If you choose to disregard this principle, you will end up finding the latter to be true in your life. In fact, I had a person in my life who would always say things like, "Just my luck," whenever some unfortunate thing would happen to them. On the contrary, I have other people in my life who always say, "Favor!" whenever good fortune happens to them.

The negative friend would never find the front door parking spots, they would always lose something valuable like their wallet or keys, and it just seemed like life was against them entirely. My positive friend, however, would always get the parking space near the front doors. Good things would seem to be following them everywhere they go, and life was their friend! There's so much more to this than just getting a good parking spot, but if you're like me in the slightest, the small things add up in life.

This book aims to help you transform your thought life through God's Word. By renewing your mind, you will learn to guard your thoughts, embrace true humility, develop a Christ-esteemed mentality, debunk some misconceptions about some common Christian subjects, and so much more that can radically change your life. The journey you are about to embark on is one of transformation, leading to a victorious, Christ-centered life.

My prayer for you as you read this book is that you will begin to renew your mind to God's Word and discover the abundant life that Jesus promised us. You were not created to live this life as a defeated person. To experience true victory and success, we need to do some mind surgery and let God's Word transform us from one thought to another.

- Matthew Ochoa

Chapter 1

The Root of All Grief

Did you know that your mind is the most powerful tool you have access to? Some of the most powerful men and women alive today all have a common denominator: their minds. I'm not talking about mind control; what I am talking about is learning how to use your own mind to your benefit.

We can look to God's Word to verify this truth. In fact, in the book of Proverbs, it says,

> *For as he thinks in his heart, so is he.*
>
> **Proverbs 23:7**

Your life is going in the direction of your most dominant thought. If you look at your current circumstances and how your life is panning out, it all comes down to how you think. You can experience a victorious life or a defeated life simply based on how your thoughts are programmed.

This is why guarding what you put in your mind is a vital part of the Christian life. Unfortunately, not many Christians have understood this truth and are suffering because of it.

If we aren't careful with what we allow into our minds, it can affect us negatively.

Your mind is where you think, imagine, dream, and understand. When I was younger, my parents never let me watch horror films. I used to think they were too strict on me. All of my friends were allowed to watch them, and they seemed perfectly fine. Somehow, I do remember watching a movie that I knew I shouldn't have been watching, and that night I would have nightmares! I even remember watching Walt Disney's Silly Symphony cartoon, The Three Little Pigs, which was made in 1933! The show wasn't scary in and of itself, but for some odd reason, the Big Bad Wolf always gave me the creeps.

I still vividly remember a nightmare that I had as a small child about the Big Bad Wolf from this cartoon coming out from under my bed and snatching me up. I can confidently say that I had never had that type of dream before I saw that cartoon, but I digress. If we aren't careful with what we allow into our minds, it can affect us negatively.

> *Keep your heart with all diligence, For out of it spring the issues of life.*
>
> **Proverbs 4:23**

According to Strong's Definitions, the word "keep" is the Hebrew word *nāṣar*, which means to guard in a good sense (to protect, maintain, obey, etc.). When I think of a guard, I tend to think of a gatekeeper who watches over a kingdom. A gatekeeper keeps things out that don't belong in and keeps things in that don't belong out. This is how we should be regarding what we allow in our minds.

When it says that we should guard our "heart," it still refers to a part of our mind. God made us as three-part beings. We are a spirit, we have a soul, and we live in a body. The soul part of us comprises our mind, will, and emotions. In Proverbs 4:23, the heart, I believe, is the combination of a man's spirit and soul.

Believe it or not, when you become born-again, your soul and your body do not change immediately. If you weren't smart before you got saved, you won't be smart after you get saved. The way we change our thought life is through the process of renewing our minds (Romans 12:2), and this is the most important thing every Christian needs to understand.

PRIDE IS THE ROOT OF ALL GRIEF

There's a reason why at the middle of the word *pride* is the letter "I." When you're all wrapped up in yourself, you'll discover that you're a really small package. Pride doesn't only mean that you think extremely highly of yourself, but it can also mean the polar opposite. Many times, people who are too shy to talk or afraid to give a presentation operate with just as much pride as the person who boasts about how great they are.

They are different ends on the same stick–pride. They are both so absorbed with their "self" that nothing else matters. The arrogant person only looks at their superior ability, and the timid person only looks at their inferior ability. It's only when we take our eyes off of ourselves completely that we can leave pride behind.

> *Only by pride cometh contention: but with the well advised is wisdom.*
>
> **Proverbs 13:10 KJV**

This is such an amazing truth. Contention doesn't come because of what someone did to you. When your pride gets hurt, contention follows. This means that you don't stop people from hurting you to control your anger issues; you have to deal with the root problem, which is your pride.

When you're so absorbed with yourself in a negative or positive way, you are prone to experience depression, stress, anxiety, and many other forms of hardship because they all deal with self-centeredness. Truly humble people don't think about themselves as better or worse than what God says about them. If you would stop being self-centered, it wouldn't matter what people said or thought about you, you're secure in what the Creator of the universe thinks about you. You could be confident and secure in who you are.

Now, there is a difference between being pridefully arrogant and being confident. In fact, the Bible often discusses how we need confidence as believers, and this confidence is always founded upon who we are in Christ. Abraham was fully convinced that God was able to perform the promises that He had made to Abraham (Romans 4:21). Being fully convinced means you are assured of it. In other words, Abraham was confident in God's ability.

Operating in arrogance, however, is when you place your confidence in yourself. You cannot operate in humility when you are being arrogant but it is very possible to be humble while being confident simultaneously.

Godly humility does not look like what most people think. For example, in the Book of Numbers, it says,

> *Now the man Moses was very humble, more than all men who were on the face of the earth.*
>
> **Numbers 12:3**

Guess who wrote this awesome statement about Moses? It was Moses! How can someone claim that they are the most humble man to ever live on earth without being prideful? It's because God told him to write it, so he did. If God were to ask the average Christian to say the same thing about themself, they would respond to God, "I can't write this about myself, God. What will everyone think of me?"

Meekness is not weakness, and humility is not self-hatred. The church has really messed up this concept. I once heard a story of a pastor telling his congregation that if anyone can claim to be the most humble person in the room, they can come up and receive a big red pin that said "HUMBLE" on it. After a few moments, one brave gentleman raised his hand and was called to come on stage. He walked up the stairs, and they pinned the button on his shirt.

As he was walking off, they told him to wait while they ripped that button off and said, "You're not humble. If you were really humble, you wouldn't have raised your hand!"

SELF-ESTEEM < CHRIST-ESTEEM

It's important that we understand true humility and how to have confidence without falling into pride. I am very confident. Not in my own ability but in who I am in Jesus. No one can take that away from me. If every believer would start adopting this type of mindset that I call being "Christ-esteemed," there wouldn't be so much division in the body of Christ.

If there's anything I've learned being in the Word, it's that we need to operate differently from how the people of the world operate. One of the biggest driving factors in the world is putting yourself first before others. This is really selfishness disguised as "self-care" or "treating yourself." Jesus demonstrated a life completely opposite to that. He always put others before Himself.

Again, humility is not self-hatred, and confidence is not prideful. These things need to be balanced. For example, I exercise frequently, eat the right things, spend time in fellowship with God, and love my wife and kids. I wouldn't go as far as to call that self-care; I'm just living my life. However, I don't go as far as Lebron James and spend millions of dollars on my physical body each year. Whether you like him or not, that is total self-absorption. When you're so full of yourself, there is no room to be full of anything else.

When you're so full of yourself, there is no room to be full of anything else.

When Jesus told us to love our neighbor as we love ourselves (Mark 12:31), this doesn't mean that we can't love others unless we love ourselves first. I've heard that interpretation from way too many high-profile pastors. If we are being honest, we all know how to love ourselves pretty well. We already know how to put our needs before others. No one has to tell us how to do that.

Jesus showed that we need to love other people in the same way we know how to love ourselves. An example of this is when you get a bonus at work. Instead of spending that money on that new flatscreen for yourself, how about you buy it for your friend or family member who you know can't afford it?

The intrusive thought might pop into your head, saying, "I worked for this. Why should I give it to someone else?" But that's your opportunity to love someone as you love yourself.

Jesus was the best example of how to love others before yourself. The whole purpose of Jesus' coming to the earth was for others–including you. I believe Jesus was able to demonstrate this trait because He was confident in His position with God. If we can learn to transition our mindset from self-centered to Christ-centered, our joy will remain even in adversity.

So, what does it mean to be "Christ-esteemed?" In its simplest form, I believe it focuses on Jesus more than you focus on anything else. Look at what the author of Hebrews wrote,

> *Therefore, since we are surrounded by such a huge crowd of witnesses to the life of faith, let us strip off every weight that slows us down, especially the sin that so easily trips us up. And let us run with endurance the race God has set before us.* ***We do this by keeping our eyes on Jesus,*** *the champion who initiates and perfects our faith...*
>
> **Hebrews 12:1-2 NLT, emphasis added**

We run our race not by looking at others and certainly not by looking at ourselves. It is done solely by looking to Jesus. If you can keep Jesus as the focus point, the end goal, the big enchilada, you can cross that finish line strong. Many Christians will be crossing that finish line while limping or crawling. Don't let that be you.

CHAPTER 1 DISCUSSION:

1. According to Proverbs 23:7, our lives follow our dominant thoughts. How can you actively steer your thoughts towards positive, faith-filled directions in your daily life?
2. Proverbs 4:23 instructs us to guard our hearts diligently, for from it flow the issues of life. How can you practically guard your mind against negative influences or thoughts that do not align with God's truth?
3. How does the distinction between pride and confidence impact your daily interactions and your relationship with God? Reflect on a recent situation where humility or confidence in Christ made a difference.
4. What steps can you take to shift your focus from self-centeredness to Christ-centeredness in your daily decisions and priorities, aligning more closely with Hebrews 12:1-2?
5. How can you practically demonstrate selfless love, as Jesus did, by considering others' needs as important as your own? Think of a specific opportunity where you can put this principle into action.

REFLECT ON WHAT THE HOLY SPIRIT SPOKE TO YOU IN THIS CHAPTER:

Chapter 2

Having Perfect Peace

As I mentioned earlier, the root of all grief is pride, which is being full of yourself. If you don't keep your focus on Jesus, it will hurt you in the long run. Look at the disciple of Jesus, Peter, for example. Many people highly esteem Peter for being the "rock" of the church. But did you know that Peter had so many shortcomings simply because he was self-centered?

For instance, Jesus and the disciples were at the tail end of their ministry tour of Galilee. Jesus taught many parables that day, including the parable of the sower found in Mark chapter 4. That parable is the most important parable to understand as a believer. It deals specifically with hardship and affliction and why bad things happen to people.

After this, Jesus gets news that His cousin, John the Baptist, was beheaded by Herod the Tetrarch. On the same day, Jesus feeds about 5,000 men (not including women and children). Finally, Jesus commanded His disciples to get into a boat and cross over the sea of Galilee.

As the disciples were crossing, Jesus went to a mountaintop to pray and saw the disciples in the middle of the sea with a storm against them. They were struggling to keep the boat afloat when Jesus went to them, walking on the water. As He approached the boat, they saw Jesus and thought He was some sort of ghost.

> *And Peter answered Him and said, Lord, if it is You, command me to come to You on the water. So He said, Come. And when Peter had come down out of the boat, he walked on the water to go to Jesus.* ***But when he saw that the wind was boisterous, he was afraid;*** *and beginning to sink he cried out, saying, Lord, save me! And immediately Jesus stretched out His hand and caught him, and said to him, O you of little faith, why did you doubt? And when they got into the boat, the wind ceased.*
>
> **Matthew 14:28-32, emphasis added**

I don't know about you, but I've never seen anyone in my entire life begin to sink. You either sink or float. The way that Matthew describes this event is awesome because it shows us that in our Christian life, we never just sink. Like Peter, we begin to sink. Peter asked Jesus to call him out on the water, and he actually began to walk on top of the water.

Peter walked on top of the very thing that was threatening their lives—what an incredible revelation. He only did this because of Jesus, who was at the center of his attention. As long as Peter was fixated on Jesus, he could walk on that water. However, the moment that Peter took his eyes off of Jesus and "saw that the wind was boisterous," he began to sink.

Think about this for a moment. What did the boisterous (or strong) wind have to do with him walking on the water? Nothing! It could have been the calmest and most peaceful day, but walking on the water would still be impossible. However, when he looked at the wind, he shifted his focus away from Jesus and became more concerned with his natural circumstances.

You will keep him in perfect peace, whose mind is stayed on You, because he trusts in You.

Isaiah 26:3

It is very possible to be in the worst circumstances yet be in perfect peace. The phrase perfect peace in the original Hebrew is "shalom, shalom." It's a peace that is so perfect, that it needs to be said twice. There is a criterion to experiencing this type of peace, and it's keeping your mind focused on Jesus. Let's break it down from the end to the beginning.

Because this person trusts in Jesus, this person will keep their mind fixated on Jesus, which will result in that person being kept in perfect peace.

The root question of all of this is how much do you trust in Jesus? You can't trust someone who you don't know. So the real question is, do you know the true nature of God? I have a teaching entitled, *Is God Out To Get Me?: Discovering the Truth About God's Nature,* which I would highly encourage you to pick up. If you don't know God's true character and nature, it will be nearly impossible to live a peaceful life.

USE YOUR SMARTPHONE'S CAMERA TO SCAN THIS QR CODE TO RECEIVE THAT TEACHING.

Jesus told us that in this life, we would have tribulation (John 16:33). The Christian life is not an escape from hardship but an empowerment to overcome every hardship. This can only be achieved when one is Christ-centered. As Hebrews 12 says, we must look to Jesus if we want to finish this race with endurance. We can't look to our friends, family members, or pastors to get us across the finish line. We need to only look to Jesus.

There have been great men and women of God who conquered the world by preaching the Gospel. Many of them healed hundreds of thousands of people in their ministry. Yet, out of those great men and women of God, many of them exited this life prematurely through sickness, and some of them squandered the calling on their lives because of a scandal. Both instances are a tragedy.

We need to stop giving people a place in our lives that only Jesus should occupy.

When people look to other people to determine what they believe in the Christian life, it will stunt them because people are imperfect in their flesh. One man that I knew preached the Gospel to the entire content of Africa, so it seemed, healing so many people of incurable diseases, yet sadly, he passed from an illness himself. Many people looked at him and said, "If it happened to him, surely it'll happen to us too." This is a result of people looking to man and not to Jesus.

Jesus is the author and finisher of our faith—not our parents, not our favorite minister, or anyone else. We need to stop giving people a place in our lives that only Jesus should occupy. The only way we can remain in peace is by keeping our minds focused on Jesus because we trust *Him* and *Him* only.

RENEWING THE MIND AND DENYING SELF

I didn't say that it was easy, but I am saying that it's necessary for a victorious life. Your emotions follow your thoughts. So, if you can keep Jesus at the center of your thoughts, your emotions will follow suit. If you operate like Peter did while walking on the water and look to things that don't matter, your emotions will follow those thoughts instead, which will lead to anxiety, fear, depression, discouragement, and the list can go on.

This is hard for many people because we have let our flesh or natural circumstances dominate us for decades. The flesh deals with five senses: see, touch, taste, smell, and hear. When was the last time you told your flesh to do anything? The answer is most likely never. Your flesh tells you when to go to bed, when to use the bathroom, when to eat, and keep eating, and keep eating.

Your flesh says when to lie down because it's not feeling well. It tells you when someone upsets you and that you need to retaliate against them. It also tells you to be sad when someone is mean to you, or someone passes away. The flesh has been controlling people for far too long but you can make that stop today.

You can take back your authority and tell your flesh what to do instead of it being the other way around. Look at what Paul says in Romans,

> *I beseech you therefore, brethren, by the mercies of God, that you present your bodies a living sacrifice, holy, acceptable to God, which is your reasonable service. And do not be conformed to this world, but be transformed by the renewing of your mind, that you may prove what is that good and acceptable and perfect will of God.*
>
> **Romans 12:1-2**

Paul starts this letter by saying, "Look, guys, this is the least that you can do in the Kingdom of God." Being a living sacrifice means that we have to put our flesh on the altar every single day. If we look away for a split second, that flesh crawls off the altar, making a break for it out the door! Why? Because the flesh doesn't want to do it. The flesh doesn't like being sacrificed. The flesh wants what the flesh wants.

In fact, I like how The Message paraphrases this scripture. It says, *"Take your everyday, ordinary life—your sleeping, eating, going-to-work, and walking-around life—and place it before God as an offering"* (Romans 12:1 MSG). The way that we sacrifice our flesh daily is by allowing what our spirit wants to do instead. Let me encourage you by saying that even Jesus had to fight His flesh. Jesus needed the same strength that we need to conquer His flesh daily.

> *Watch and pray, lest you enter into temptation. The spirit indeed is willing, but the flesh is weak.*
>
> **Matthew 26:41**

Jesus was in the Garden of Gathesemen on the night of His arrest, and He asked His disciples to stay awake with Him and pray. When He got back, He found them asleep. Many people believe that Jesus was saying what He said in this verse because of their lack of commitment to stay awake, but I believe Jesus was referring to Himself. After all three times, He prayed, "O My Father, if it is possible, let this cup pass from Me; nevertheless, not as I will, but as You will."

Our born-again spirits are always ready to do what God wants us to do, but it's our flesh that causes problems. When Jesus spoke about the "flesh," He didn't only mean our physical bodies but also our souls (where our mind resides). God has given each of us all that we need to experience a victorious life, but "we have this treasure in earthen vessels" (2 Corinthians 4:7). That means our born-again spirits, where God has placed all His power and glory, are confined within our flesh.

However, this doesn't mean we can't access this power. When we renew our minds (Romans 12:2) and act on God's Word (James 2:20), we can actually experience this power and see it come to pass in our lives. Just as physical muscles must be exercised to grow stronger, our souls and physical bodies must be trained (1 Timothy 4:7-8).

Being conformed to the world means falling into the trap of esteeming one's own accomplishments. Instead, we are to be transformed by renewing our minds to God's Word. The first thing we need to renew our minds to is Romans 12, verse 3.

> *For I say, through the grace given to me, to everyone who is among you, not to think of himself more highly than he ought to think, but to think soberly, as God has dealt to each one a measure of faith.*
>
> **Romans 12:3**

We are told not to think of ourselves more highly than we ought to think. Evidently, there is a right way and a wrong way to think of ourselves. Again, we aren't trying to hate ourselves, but we also don't want to esteem ourselves more than what is right. Where is the balance? Instead of thinking too highly or puffed up, we must think soberly about ourselves, and this is the determining factor: **as God has dealt with each one as a measure of faith.**

In the King James Version, it reads, "God hath dealt to every man *the* measure of faith." I like this version the best because it aligns with the overarching theme of faith in the Bible. God has given each of us *the* measure of faith. It's one measure for everyone.

Imagine standing in a soup line waiting for your bowl to be filled. God is standing there at the pot of faith with His ladle, and He's pouring one measure of faith into everyone's bowl that passes. A lot of times, we get tripped up by the terms "more faith" or "little faith," but in reality, we all have the same exact measure.

Let's go back to the muscle analogy. Faith is also like a muscle. In our physical bodies, we have all the muscles we would ever need to look like Arnold Schwarzenegger or Dwyane "The Rock" Johnson. If I wanted to, I could look like either of those guys. I just don't want to. I have the potential because I have the muscles. Likewise, we all have the same faith that Jesus had while He was on the earth.

> *I am crucified with Christ: nevertheless I live; yet not I, but Christ liveth in me: and the life which I now live in the flesh* ***I live by the faith of the Son of God****, who loved me, and gave himself for me.*
>
> **Galatians 2:20 KJV**

Just because you possess all the faith you'll ever need doesn't mean that you use all of it. Again, faith is like a muscle; if it's never used, it never grows. God has given us a level playing field regarding faith and all that faith can accomplish in our lives. Some people use more of that faith than others, but we all started at ground zero.

The moment we begin to esteem ourselves above others (especially in the area of faith), we will fall flat on our backs. Pride always comes before the fall (Proverbs 16:18). Look at Muhammed Ali, a.k.a. The Greatest of All Time. He would appear in all the news tabloids and TV interviews saying, "I am the greatest!" repeatedly. Sadly, his life was diminished when he developed Young-Onset Parkinson's just three years after his retirement. I don't care how great you think you are; pride will always come before the fall.

YOU GOTTA GIVE IT UP

Another crucial aspect of not being conformed to the world is not letting your own desires and wants overpower God's will for your life. If that is the case, then we need to deny ourselves completely.

> *Do not love the world or the things in the world. If anyone loves the world, the love of the Father is not in him. For all that is in the world—the lust of the flesh, the lust of the eyes, and the pride of life—is not of the Father but is of the world.*
>
> 1 John 2:15-16

This doesn't mean that you can never enjoy the things that the world offers. God created the world for our benefit and for our enjoyment. The issue lies when you start worshipping the creation instead of the Creator. Many people have a hard time accepting this truth because they are too in love with their flesh and what their flesh desires.

I've heard stories of people putting God's plans on hold because they are waiting to retire from their jobs with the most they can get. I've also heard stories of people completely forsaking the things of God because of some worldly dream they are chasing. Either way, they both have the same issue: loving the things of the world more than loving the things of God.

Our goal is not to hate ourselves but to view ourselves in light of how God views us.

Notice the three ways the world offers things to us: the lust of the flesh, the lust of the eyes, and the pride of life. The lust of the flesh deals with things that you want to consume. It can be as little as eating an apple to replenish your body or sleeping around every night to fulfill a sexual desire.

The lust of the eyes has to do with things that look desirable. For example, when Abram and Lot parted ways in Genesis, Lot went to the area of Sodom and Gomorrah because it looked well-watered and green (Genesis 13:10). It was pleasing to the eye. We all know the outcome of that decision.

Lastly, there is the pride of life. This can deal with one's status or ego or, more simply, self-esteem. The dictionary defines self-esteem as "Pride in one's own worth or abilities; self-respect" (Oxford's Dictionary).

The synonyms for self-esteem are ego, pride, pridefulness, self-regard, and self-respect. Our goal is not to hate ourselves but to view ourselves in light of how God views us. We shouldn't be so focused on what man thinks about us. Our worth comes from Jesus. After all, Jesus paid for us. Someone might purchase something that others would find worthless. Have you ever heard someone say, "That is not worth it"?

Right now, the real estate market is inflated with homes that are selling way above their actual value, but people are still buying them. Why? It's worth it to them. It might not be worth it to bystanders, but it's worth it to people who have bought the home. No one can determine your value other than the one who bought you, Jesus. You might try to place a value on yourself, but if you aren't seeing yourself through the eyes of Jesus, you'll miss it every time.

The world will try to offer you things to boost your self-esteem, but it won't last. Once that wears off, it'll offer you something else, something "better" than before. Stop valuing what the world offers you and start valuing what Jesus offers you.

I've mentioned him before, and I'll keep mentioning him. The Apostle Paul had a great understanding of this. This is what he says in Romans,

For I know that in me (that is, in my flesh) nothing good dwells...

Romans 7:18

Nothing in ourselves, our accomplishments, or our desires is worthy of esteem. But when we place ourselves in Jesus, that is where our value comes from. When we see how much God loves us and what Jesus did for us on the cross, we will begin to truly flourish.

Then Jesus said to His disciples, If anyone desires to come after Me, let him deny himself, and take up his cross, and follow Me. For whoever desires to save his life will lose it, but whoever loses his life for My sake will find it.

Matthew 16:24-25

A cross is something that we die on. When you deny yourself, what you're saying is, "It's not my own accomplishments. It's not about me anymore. I'm denying my own pleasures, my own ambitions, what I think is true and relying on what God's Word says." That takes faith. There are a lot of people today who think they know what is best for themselves, but if it's not rooted in God's love for them, they're wrong.

Some people would even say, "But I don't want to give up my own pleasures. I like my life. I don't want to change anything." As long as you can continue to live your life without God, you will. God won't force His plans for your life on you.

If anyone comes to Me and does not hate his father and mother, wife and children, brothers and sisters, yes, and his own life also, he cannot be My disciple. And whoever does not bear his cross and come after Me cannot be My disciple.

Luke 14:26-27

We should hate our own family relative to our commitment to God. People today are too afraid to step out in faith and listen to God's instructions because they fear what their families will think of them. That is the pride of life written all over their hearts. They love what people think about them more than they love the things of God.

Mastering our thoughts, understanding true humility, and renewing our minds is fundamental to living a victorious Christian life.

Paul says in Romans that we should let God's Word be absolute truth in our lives, and everything else should be a lie (Romans 3:4). That is how big our commitment to what God says about us should be over everything else. Mastering our thoughts, understanding true humility, and renewing our minds is fundamental to living a victorious Christian life. As we look to Jesus and rely on His strength, we can overcome any challenge and live out the abundant life He promised.

CHAPTER 2 DISCUSSION:

1. How can you apply the principle of keeping your mind fixed on Jesus to overcome challenges and maintain inner peace in your daily life?
2. Reflecting on the story of Peter walking on water, how does it illustrate the importance of faith and focus on Jesus amidst life's storms? What distractions threaten your focus on Jesus?
3. In what ways can you actively renew your mind according to Romans 12:1-2, especially in areas where worldly desires and self-centeredness may conflict with God's will?

REFLECT ON WHAT THE HOLY SPIRIT SPOKE TO YOU IN THIS CHAPTER:

Chapter 3

Change "I Can't" To "I Can"

I want to take us back to the first scripture I mentioned at the start of this book.

> *For as he thinks in his heart, so is he.*
>
> **Proverbs 23:7**

It takes a huge amount of responsibility to realize that you are in control of the direction of your life. The Bible doesn't say, "as a godly man thinks in his heart" or "as a wicked person thinks in his heart." This principle applies to everyone with a breath in their lungs and a heart beating in their chest.

We all need to see ourselves as God sees us through the eyes of Jesus. We need to be encouraged whenever we think about ourselves. Most Christians consider themselves to be nothing and to have nothing, but if you have Jesus, you have, and you are everything. If you can change how you think from a loser to a victor in Christ, you will see victory in your life. God is so good that He gave us a simple solution to how we experience life, and it's through how we think.

THE POWER OF THE MIND

I mentioned earlier that the mind is the most powerful tool you can access on this earth. It's so powerful that in the Bible, there is a story that shows God being threatened by mankind's imagination.

> *And the Lord said, Behold, the people is one, and they have all one language; and this they begin to do: and now nothing will be restrained from them, which they have imagined to do.*
>
> **Genesis 11:6 KJV**

After the flood, Noah and his family were the next generation. The descendants of Noah decided to build a tower that would reach the sky for two main reasons. Firstly, they wanted to be remembered and praised for achieving something remarkable. Secondly, they wanted to keep everyone united in one place (Genesis 11:4).

There are a few reasons why God was threatened by them, but one of the main reasons is that they all set their minds to it. They were united in their minds. There is certainly power in unity to do good, but there is also power in unity to do evil.

A common trait that you will find in most successful and influential leaders is the ability to cast a vision and have the people buy into that vision. Look at Adolf Hitler. He was able to persuade an entire nation to follow his lead. How did he do that?

> **"He learned how to become a charismatic speaker, and people, for whatever reason, became enamored with him. People were most willing to follow him because he seemed to have the right answers in a time of enormous economic upheaval"** (Professor Bruce Loebs, Business Insider).

He rallied people by the thousands and gave them a vision. Now, this isn't a history lesson about Nazi Germany, but he was undoubtedly one of the most influential leaders ever to lead. Unfortunately, his leadership was one of evil and wickedness.

Another example that is more positive is our yearly Big Vision Sunday, which we hold annually at the start of every year at Deep Rooted Church. Each year, we look at what God did in the previous year and what He wants to do in the upcoming year, and we present this to our church. Because we are united in what we believe God wants to do in the church, great things get accomplished. Whether I used good or bad examples, the point is that there is power in unity, especially unity in the mind.

Man's ability to accomplish anything begins in the mind–specifically the imagination. Andrew Wommack has a great teaching called *The Power of Imagination*. In it, he writes,

> **"Your imagination is like your spiritual womb. It's your creative center"** (Andrew Wommack, The Power of Imagination, 2019, p. 8).

He describes the imagination as a spiritual womb because Isaiah 26:3 and Genesis 6:5 share the same Hebrew word, *yêtser*, which is literally translated as "conception" (Strong's Concordance). This is how an artist paints a beautiful work of art. Every stroke of the brush and every blend of the colors originates in the mind. If you can't see it in your mind, you can't accomplish it physically.

This is why we need to start seeing ourselves the way God sees us and think about ourselves in that same light. If man's imagination threatened God's plans for mankind so that He had to intervene and limit man's ability to communicate, then imagination is powerful, and we need to use it for His glory.

One way that you begin doing this is by changing your mindset from "I can't" to "I can." I grew up in a Mexican household with Mexican grandparents from both sides of my parents. One common phrase I heard while growing up was, "You're a Mexi**can**, not Mexi-**can't**!"

Whenever you find yourself doing something difficult and the thought tries to tell you that you can't do it, you need to counter it by saying I can do it. I've developed a habit in my life to tell myself, "I can do hard things," the moment I find myself wanting to give up or quit. I've seen myself accomplish many things since then because of what I believe about myself. But here's the caveat: I'm encouraging myself because of who I know I am in Jesus.

TRUST JESUS IN DIFFICULT TIMES

I'm not just saying I can do hard things just to say them. I truly believe it. And I believe it because of what I believe God thinks about me. I believe that God created me to be able to do hard things. I know and am fully convinced that God created me to be victorious in life. The head and not the tail, up front and never lagging behind. That is who I am in Christ!

> *I can do all things through Christ who strengthens me.*
>
> **Philippians 4:13**

Paul wasn't saying that he can do all things through himself. It was only through Jesus that he could do the things he did. This is one of the most taken-out-of-context verses in the Bible. You'll find this on football helmets or tattooed onto a UFC fighter's back.

People don't see this verse's true value because it's been misused and abused. Paul wasn't telling us that we can do whatever we want to do in life. I'm not telling you that, either. If what you're trying to do isn't through the grace that God gave you through Jesus, you won't have the strength to do it.

In the context of Paul's writings, he was dealing with hardship and persecution from his ministry. Paul was left for dead, beaten, shipwrecked, bitten by a poisonous snake, whipped, starving, freezing in the cold, and so many more horrible things for preaching the Gospel.

Through the lack and the hardship that he was experiencing, he was saying that he could suffer it and go through it because he could do all things through Christ, who gave him strength. He was not saying, "I can score this touchdown because Jesus gave me the strength to do so." However, the same power that sustains Paul to suffer the hardship of the ministry is the same power that enables us to live a victorious life!

> *Therefore I take pleasure in infirmities, in reproaches, in needs, in persecutions, in distresses, for Christ's sake. For when I am weak, then I am strong.*
>
> **2 Corinthians 12:10**

Paul found joy in his hardships, not because they felt pleasant or because he thought God inflicted them. He found joy in them because he understood that enduring these challenges meant he was headed in the right direction. It's only when we recognize that we are weak in our flesh that we can find strength in Christ.

Once you realize that you can't handle it alone, you can tap into the strength and power that Jesus has given you. When you reach the point of saying, "I've reached my limit and can't do this anymore," that's when you can draw on God's strength. Then, you can begin to change your "I can't" to "I can."

CHAPTER 3 DISCUSSION:

1. How does my view of myself align with God's perspective of me? How can I change my mindset from "I Can't" to "I Can" in who I am in Christ? (Proverbs 23:7)
2. In what areas of my life am I limiting God's work through negative thinking or lack of vision? How can I harness the power of imagination and unity of purpose to pursue God's plans and purposes more effectively? (Genesis 11:6)
3. Reflecting on Philippians 4:13, how can I apply the principle of relying on Christ's strength in my daily challenges and responsibilities? How does this perspective shift from personal empowerment to reliance on God's grace?
4. When faced with difficulties or doubts, how can I cultivate a habit of speaking faith-filled declarations over myself, aligning them with God's promises? (Philippians 4:13, 2 Corinthians 12:10)
5. What practical steps can I take to renew my mind daily with God's Word, ensuring that my thoughts and imagination are aligned with His truth and promises? How can this transformation impact my outlook on life and my ability to fulfill God's purposes?

REFLECT ON WHAT THE HOLY SPIRIT SPOKE TO YOU IN THIS CHAPTER:

Chapter 4

Get A Word From God

When Paul traveled the world preaching the Gospel, he often needed financial assistance. At one point, he operated a small tent-making business to help provide the necessary funds for traveling and lodging. However, that wasn't God's best for his life.

In his letter to the Philippians, Paul thanked them for how they had ministered to him in his life. Apparently, they had desired to bless Paul for some time, but they lacked the opportunity to do so. They couldn't communicate the way we communicate today. If you wanted to send me a blessing, you could text me or message me on social media and I would be able to communicate where you could send the gift. That wasn't the way they did things in Paul's day.

At this point in his life, Paul had been imprisoned for over two years, shipwrecked, and rejected by many people. However, he still considered himself to be full and abounding (Philippians 4:18). This is because Paul found contentment in who he was in the Lord, not in material things or in people's opinions.

While he was thanking the Philippians for their generosity, he gave them a word that is still powerful and true today.

> *And my God shall supply all your need according to His riches in glory by Christ Jesus.*
>
> **Philippians 4:19**

What an amazing promise! God will supply *all* your needs at all times, no matter what, under any circumstances? No, that's not what it said. If you take the text out of its context, all that you're left with is a con. Paul said that God would supply all of their needs according to *His* riches in glory *by (or through)* Christ Jesus. Once again, it's only through Jesus that we can receive these amazing blessings.

It takes faith to trust God with your money.

Now, if you want to get even more technical, Paul was giving this promise to a specific group of people–his ministry partners. Paul wasn't just saying this to anyone. The Philippians were the only ones supporting Paul and his ministry. This promise does not apply to everyone. God wants all of His children to have their needs met and supplied, but not all of His children are cooperating in giving and receiving. The promise is for those who are faithfully giving like these Philippians.

Again, of course, God wants to supply all of our needs, but we need to believe that He can! So, how do we express our faith when it comes to finances? It's through our giving. When we give, we trust that God will take better care of us with what we have left over than we can take care of ourselves while holding on to everything. It takes faith to give away your hard-earned income. It takes faith to trust God with your money.

Paul gave them a word, a promise, that God would supply all of their need because of their faith in God's provision. When you receive a word like that, you need to plant it into your heart.

If you are struggling financially, you need to seek God's word about finances and plant that word in your heart. One critical aspect of changing the way you think in life is being selective with what you hear. As Proverbs 4:23 says, "*Keep your heart with all diligence, for out of it spring the issues of life.*" We need to be very careful about what we allow in our hearts. The way that we guard our hearts is by not allowing certain things to enter our hearing.

THE POWER OF WORDS

My friend Dustin Barker has a book entitled *Change Your Words, Change Your Life*, that discusses the power of the tongue. Believe it or not, your words are powerful. They are either producing life or death. We have Dustin come to speak at our church every year and during one of his messages, he explained a cycle of how we begin to believe certain things, whether they are good or bad, about ourselves.

The cycle begins when you either experience something in your life or hear something about yourself. He said in a message in 2022,

> "They believe, 'I'm accident prone,' so what do they do? They say, 'I'm accident prone,' and because they say it, it happens. [When it happens] they aren't surprised because they've been expecting it the whole time. And when it happens, that just confirms that accidents must happen, and they are caught in the cycle." [1]

This is why it's important to guard what comes into your heart. You have to be cautious in two ways: what you say about yourself, and what you believe others say about you.

Maybe you've been told you'll never amount to anything in life. When you hear negative words repeatedly, they can start to affect your self-perception. Eventually, you will begin to internalize these comments and see yourself as a failure. This is your imagination at work; you're envisioning yourself as a loser.

Some people have dealt with a sickness or ailment for decades. Over time, the negative statements they've heard, such as "You'll never recover" or "You have to learn to live with this condition," have led

1 Dustin Barker. (2022). Change Your Words, Change Your Life [Video]. YouTube. Deep Rooted Church. https://www.youtube.com/channel/DeepRootedChurch

them to view themselves as a sick person in their mind. They aren't only sick in the body but sick in the head! Their sickness becomes the focal point of their lives–they plan their activities around it, and it dictates what they can or cannot do. What they need is a Word from God!

YOU'RE GOING TO THE OTHER SIDE

Let's recall the passage from Matthew 14 when Jesus walks on water to meet his disciples. Just before the storm struck their boat, Jesus had given his disciples a specific word.

> *Immediately Jesus made His disciples get into the boat and go before Him to the other side, while He sent the multitudes away.*
>
> **Matthew 14:22**

I find it very interesting that Jesus "made His disciples get into the boat" (Matthew 14:22). Both Matthew and Mark's accounts record Jesus having to persuade the disciples to enter the boat and cross the sea of Galilee (Mark 6:45). In fact, in the Greek text, this verse is translated in a way that shows Jesus having to compel them by force. Some of the men in this group were avid fishermen by trade. They practically lived on the sea. I could imagine that some of these men like Peter, Andrew, James, and his brother John all saw the conditions of the sea and the upcoming weather and were hesitant to go out.

It took faith for them to go against their natural instincts. Although a quotation of Jesus saying, "Go to the other side," is not recorded, it's implied through the author's writings that's what He told them to do. To get in the boat and to go to the other side of the sea. This is huge if you can understand this.

If Jesus says, "You're going to the other side," then you're going to the other side! The very fact that Jesus was implying, "I'll meet you on the other side guys" was all of the validation those disciples needed to launch out into the water and head toward the other side.

However, when they got into the middle of the sea, the storm came against them violently. The waves were beating on the boat, the water was getting in the boat and the wind was blowing against the boat. Everything was pointing against what Jesus told them. Oftentimes in our lives, when we receive a Word from God, the enemy will try all that he can to derail us from that promise by sending something contrary to His Word.

DON'T LET THE DEVIL STEAL YOUR WORD

We had members in our church receive a revelation on God's healing power available to us on the inside. After they received healing, they were battling more sickness than before! What happened was that the enemy didn't want that word to be fully planted in their hearts, so he sent hardship to try to take it away.

This is exactly what is happening to the disciples. In Mark's account of this story, it says, "*Now about the fourth watch of the night He came to them*" (Mark 6:48). Earlier, we read that Jesus sent them away just before evening or sunset. The fourth watch of the night was between 3 and 6 a.m. The disciples were about eight to ten hours into crossing the Sea of Galilee before Jesus came walking to them on the water.

That's a lot of struggling for little to no results. John records, "*They had rowed about three or four miles*" (John 6:19). The average boat and rower takes about 15 to 45 minutes to travel four miles yet the disciples took much longer.

They allowed fear to triumph over the words of Jesus Himself. They had so much fear that they did everything within themselves to prevent them from dying. It even says that Jesus "*would have passed them by*" (Mark 6:48) but luckily they saw Him and thought He was a ghost. When God gives you a word, and circumstances arise that are contrary to that word, it's not your job to "make it happen." Our job is to focus on that promise. And lucky for all of us, God has given us many words to hold onto and they have all been written down in *His* Word–The Bible!

ONLY SPEAK A WORD

All you need to pass through whatever circumstance you might be facing or will encounter in the future is a word from the Lord. There are so many scriptures that give you a promise and if you were to hold onto those promises instead of embracing the word that your doctor, banker, or relative is giving you, it could change your life.

> *Now when Jesus had entered Capernaum, a centurion came to Him, pleading with Him, saying, Lord, my servant is lying at home paralyzed, dreadfully tormented. And Jesus said to him, I will come and heal him. The centurion answered and said, Lord, I am not worthy that You should come under my roof.* ***But only speak a word****, and my servant will be healed.*
>
> **Matthew 8:5-8, emphasis added**

A centurion was a captain of 100 soldiers in the Roman army. He was a person in command, yet he humbled himself and lowered himself below Jesus. This goes back to chapter 1 of this book. Humility is a vital key to understand if you want to see victory in your life. But this centurion doesn't just stop there. He says something that I wish every Christian would grab ahold of. He said, *"Only speak a word, and my servant will be healed."*

The first recorded healing is found in John 4:46. It involves a nobleman coming to Jesus because his son is dying, and he wants Jesus to come to his house to heal him. John writes, *"Jesus said to him, 'Go your way; your son lives.' So the man believed the word that Jesus spoke to him, and he went his way"* (John 4:50).

Humility is a vital key to understand if you want to see victory in your life.

Many Christians today struggle with fully believing unless they see Jesus physically do something rather than just speaking a word. Thomas, for instance, was famously labeled Doubting Thomas because he insisted on seeing Jesus in the flesh before believing that he had risen from the dead. Yet the nobleman in this story went home fully trusting in Jesus' word. He didn't require Jesus to physically lay hands on his son.

To the nobleman's credit, he believed *after* Jesus told him his child would live. However, the centurion believed *before* Jesus said anything. Jesus said that the centurion's faith was the greatest faith He ever saw (Matthew 8:10). It was a faith that was totally dependent on Jesus' words only.

Jesus has already given us His Word that by His stripes we are healed (Isaiah 53:5 & 1 Peter 2:24). If that is not enough for you to receive what God wants to give to you, then to a degree, you are operating in doubt and doubt is the killer to faith.

WHAT DOES THE WORD SAY?

My pastor, Jeremy Pearsons, likes to share a story of when he and his sister were children growing up in their home. As he says, they lived in *the* household of faith. It was faith in the morning, faith in the afternoon, and faith in the evening. They would get up every morning at 6 a.m. to watch "Papa" Copeland teach on *The Believer's Voice of Victory*.

One evening at the dinner table, his sister was discussing a current issue she was facing in her life and was looking for the right answers. After she would tell her parents what was going on, her parents would look back at her and say, "Well, what does the Word say?"

She would respond with, "No, seriously, guys. What should I do?" and they would respond back again with, "What does the Word say?"

Frustrated, she turned to her brother Jeremy at the other end of the dining table for support, only to hear the same question echoed back to her: "Well, what does the Word say?"

There has never been and will never be an issue in our lives that the Word of God doesn't have the answer to.

> *All Scripture is given by inspiration of God, and is profitable for doctrine, for reproof, for correction, for instruction in righteousness, that the man of God may be complete, thoroughly equipped for every good work.*
>
> **2 Timothy 3:16-17**

CHICKEN AND DUMPLINGS

Earlier this year, I did something very stupid, but by the grace of God, I didn't see the negative effects manifest in my life because of my foundation in what the Word of God says about me. My wife had recently made some amazing chicken and dumplings for dinner. Every few months or so, she'll make this dinner to change it up. Notice I said, "Every few months or so."

She made them on a Tuesday night, and they were as delicious as always. After dinner, she put the food away in the fridge as leftovers. We winded down for the night and went to bed. The following day, I was thinking about what to eat for lunch, and I remembered the delicious dinner I had the night before.

I went to the fridge and opened the bowl where it was stored, placed some in a bowl, and threw it in the microwave. After cooking it for a few minutes, I ate about two servings of it and went about the rest of my day, which consisted of Small Groups at our church.

The following day, I was enjoying a relaxing morning when, all of a sudden, Stephanie asked me, "Did you have chicken and dumplings yesterday?"

I responded, "Yeah, why?"

"Did you eat them from the bowl?"

"Yes...why?" my response was. At this moment I had realized I messed up, and I messed up *big time*.

Apparently, I had eaten a *few months-old* moldy chicken and dumplings that were just rotting away in the fridge. She had placed the new chicken and dumplings in a different container, and I was so hungry (and dumb) that I didn't even bother checking.

Now, I must admit, my emotions went wild. I thought I was going to die (sometimes, I am a little too dramatic). But once those emotions were reeled back in and I was thinking clearly, I started to recall what the Word says like in Mark 16:18, *"and if they drink any deadly thing, it shall not hurt them; they shall lay hands on the sick, and they shall recover."*

I truly believed that I wouldn't get sick, but if I did for some reason, I could be healed from it regardless. I also thought about the time

Paul got bitten by a poisonous snake and lived while everyone thought he was going to die (Acts 28:3-5). And because I am dramatic, I would recall scriptures like, *"I shall not die, but live, and declare the works of the Lord"* (Psalm 118:17).

This didn't happen overnight in my life, though. These scriptures have been implanted into my heart for years before this dumb accident. I had been meditating on God's Word before I faced an issue in my life. These words in the Bible are now the way I see myself. It's taken over my thought life and as a result, it has taken over my physical life too. I want to encourage you if I can get to a place where this is real in my life, so can you. And it's simply by the grace of God that I had zero symptoms of food poisoning or any other side effects from eating bad leftovers.

I was an over-dramatic person before God's Word became alive in my heart (and apparently, I'm still in the transformation process). My emotions used to control me because I would *think* about the undesired outcomes in my life. But once you can get a word from the Lord and hold onto it, you can face any challenge and triumph over it.

CHAPTER 4 DISCUSSION:

1. How can I cultivate a mindset of contentment and reliance on God's provision, similar to Paul's attitude in Philippians 4:18, amidst life's challenges and uncertainties?
2. In what ways can I exercise faith in God's promises regarding provision, especially in my financial decisions and challenges? How can I align my giving with trust in God's abundant provision, as seen in Philippians 4:19?
3. Reflecting on the story of Jesus calming the storm and walking on water (Matthew 14:22-33), how can I strengthen my faith to trust God's word over circumstances that may seem contrary to His promises?
4. Considering the power of words discussed (Proverbs 4:23, Matthew 8:5-8), how can I be more intentional in guarding what I allow into my heart and mind, especially in terms of affirming God's promises over negative self-talk or external criticisms?
5. What steps can I take to immerse myself more deeply in God's Word, so that His promises become deeply rooted in my heart and mind, providing a firm foundation in times of challenge or uncertainty (2 Timothy 3:16-17)?

REFLECT ON WHAT THE HOLY SPIRIT SPOKE TO YOU IN THIS CHAPTER:

Chapter 5

Casting Down Imaginations

The Word of God takes time to plant, nourish, and bear fruit in our lives. You can't expect it to start working after reading a few scriptures for five minutes. This is where I believe a lot of Christians get discouraged and stop pursuing the Word because they feel that it's not working in their lives.

> *And he said, So is the kingdom of God, as if a man should cast seed into the ground; and should sleep, and rise night and day, and the seed should spring and grow up, he knoweth not how. For the earth bringeth forth fruit of herself; first the blade, then the ear, after that the full corn in the ear.*
>
> **Mark 4:26-28 KJV**

When Jesus taught this parable of the sower and the seed, He was relating the seed to the Word of God (Mark 4:14). Notice the sower's job and responsibility in this parable. He's supposed to sow the seed into the ground, sleep, and rise day after day, and the seed springs up.

SEEDS TAKE TIME TO GROW

I remember that, in elementary school, my teacher would have the whole class participate in a science project that involved planting a small seed into a cup with some dirt in it. After a few weeks, we'd returned to our cup of dirt, and we all would notice a small plant sprouting out. We were learning the process of seed time and harvest (Genesis 8:22).

When we believe in something and it doesn't come to pass, we are tempted to give up.

Not all seeds grow at the same rate. Some take a short amount of time to sprout, while others take what feels like a lifetime to reach full maturity. For example, a cornflower seed can take seven to ten days to sprout, but a coconut seed may take up to four months to germinate and sprout.

1 Peter 1:23 calls God's Word an incorruptible seed living on the inside of us. The moment we plant it into our hearts, it wants to sprout, but it takes time. When we are waiting to see any sort of fruit manifest, there is a temptation to think that it's not working.

> *Hope deferred makes the heart sick, but when the desire comes, it is a tree of life.*
>
> **Proverbs 13:12**

When we believe in something in our lives, and it doesn't seem to come to pass in the timeframe that we thought it would, we are tempted to give up and quit believing. This is why it's important to guard your mind from intrusive thoughts that will try to tell lies about your situation.

BELIEVE WHILE YOU WAIT

My wife, Stephanie, and I got married in 2019. We devoted an entire year to our marriage and waited to have children. After that year, we began trying for our first child. For two years, we didn't see our dream of having a child happen.

As the man of the house and provider, I could have been tempted to give into thoughts like, "Maybe I'm infertile and can't give my wife children." Instead, my wife and I held onto the promise of the Word.

> *Behold, children are a heritage from the Lord, the fruit of the womb is a reward. Like arrows in the hand of a warrior, so are the children of one's youth. Happy is the man who has his quiver full of them; they shall not be ashamed, but shall speak with their enemies in the gate.*
>
> **Psalm 127:3-5**

> *Children's children are the crown of old men, and the glory of children is their father.*
>
> **Proverbs 17:6**

I can even recall a time when I was preaching on stage, encouraging others who were believing for a child to start preparing the nursery before they even get pregnant; all the while, that's what we were believing God for.

One couple messaged us privately (who had been trying to conceive but had great difficulties), announcing that they did what I had said to do, and they received a positive pregnancy test shortly after. We could have been discouraged that others were receiving these blessings while we were still without them, but we continued to focus on the Word, rejoiced with those who rejoiced and kept believing. Not long after, we were blessed with our firstborn son, Matthew Jr. Now, we have a strong, healthy boy and *another on the way!*

This can also apply to someone who has been believing to receive healing in their life. If you've been suffering from a sickness or ailment in your body for some time, the temptation is to give up and stop believing altogether. We've seen this happen many times in our years of pastoring, and it's very unfortunate.

Some people have been dealing with a sickness or disease for so long that not only do they no longer believe they will be healed from it, but they now identify with it. They'll say things like, "I *have* MS," or "*My* allergies are acting up," and even, "I'm believing God will take away *my* sickness." They've allowed what they're going through to now define who they are.

SPIRITUAL FIGHTS NEED SPIRITUAL WEAPONS

Paul tells us how to get rid of this type of mindset in 2 Corinthians,

> *For the weapons of our warfare are not carnal but mighty in God for pulling down strongholds, casting down arguments and every high thing that exalts itself against the knowledge of God, bringing every thought into captivity to the obedience of Christ.*
>
> **2 Corinthians 10:4-5**

In case you didn't know, we are in a spiritual battle, and this spiritual battle isn't fought and won with physical means but spiritual means. The woman with the issue of blood in Mark 5 is a great example of this. She "had a flow of blood for twelve years" (Mark 5:25) and went to every doctor she could afford, but it got worse instead of better.

Adam Clarke describes in his commentary what kind of remedies were prescribed to this woman:

> Take of gum Alexandria, of alum, and of crocus hortensis, the weight of a zuzee each; let them be bruised together, and given in wine to the woman that hath an issue of blood. But if this fail, Take of Persian onions nine logs, boil them in wine, and give it to her to drink: and say, Arise from thy flux. But should this fail, Set her in a place where two ways meet, and let her hold a cup of wine in her hand; and let somebody come behind and affright her, and say, Arise from thy flux. But should this do no good, Take a handful of cummin and a handful of crocus, and a handful of faenu-greek; let these be boiled, and given her to drink, and say, Arise from thy flux. But should this also fail, Dig seven trenches, and burn in them some cuttings of vines not yet circumcised (vines not four years old); and let her take in her hand a cup of wine, and let her be led from this trench and set down over that, and let her be removed

from that, and set down over another: and in each removal say unto her, Arise from thy flux. [1]

Not only did she spend all that she had on doctors and medicine, but she was humiliated and tormented for nothing. It wasn't until she heard that Jesus was in town and He had a sure cure for her ailment that she received her healing. She tried to use physical means to heal herself, but all she truly needed was Jesus.

Many Christians today would do well spending the same amount of time, money, and energy in the Word, Bible Studies, or anything else to receive healing as they do on naturally, worldy remedies like medical expenses. If Christians had no access to healthcare, I believe we would have no other choice than to fully commit ourselves to the healing power of God's Word instead of spending on doctor's visits and hospital bills. I'm not against doctors, but I am against our dependency on them *over* the Word of God. We are fighting a spiritual battle, and we can't depend on physical things to win. We can absolutely use physical things, but we should never depend on them.

> *For the weapons of our warfare are not carnal but mighty in God for pulling down strongholds.*
>
> **2 Corinthians 10:4**

We have weapons (plural) at our disposal to fight this spiritual battle, and we need to access them. With these weapons, we are able to actively resist and fight against the devil and his attacks in our lives (James 4:7). Notice what these weapons are specifically designed to do: ***they pull down strongholds.***

STRONGHOLDS: DEFENSE MECHANISMS

A stronghold is a defense mechanism that people run behind when they become offended. Many times in the past, I would get pushback

1 Clarke, A. (1831). The Holy Bible containing the Old and New Testaments, with a commentary and critical notes. J. Emory and B. Waugh.

from religious leaders in the area about some of the things I would say and preach on. There was this one time when a very prominent man in the church I was involved with publicly came out against me over certain things I would say online.

He would be quiet until I started talking about healing in the Bible. In fact, healing is one of the most trigger-sensitive topics to talk about, I've noticed. I would say simple truths found in God's Word, like it's always God's will for us to be healed and that we have the same raising from the dead power living on the inside of us. Simple Bible 101 stuff (at least for our church, it is).

The interesting thing was that whenever I shared about finances, emotions, or anything else unrelated to healing, this guy would respond with crickets—not a single word. But the moment I mentioned healing, it was like I slapped his mom in the face or something!

The Lord showed me what I was dealing with. At first, I was tempted to lash out at the guy and tell him what I thought of him, but the Lord reminded me of this scripture. *"For we do not wrestle against flesh and blood, but against principalities, against powers, against the rulers of the darkness of this age, against spiritual hosts of wickedness in the heavenly places"* (Ephesians 6:12).

My fight wasn't with this guy. My fight was with something influencing his aggression. It was a stronghold that I was fighting. See, the word "strongholds" in the Greek is *ochýrōma*, and it means "of the arguments and reasonings by which a disputant endeavors to fortify his opinion and defend it against his opponent." [2]

A stronghold is like a mental fortress made from arguments and reasoning.

A stronghold is like a mental vfortress made from arguments and reasoning. People use it to support their opinions and protect them from being challenged by others. The moment you talk about a touchy subject with that person, in-

2 G3794 - Ochyrōma - Strong's Greek lexicon (KJV). Blue Letter Bible. (n.d.). https://www.blueletterbible.org/lexicon/g3794/kjv/tr/0-1/

stantly, their walls go up, and they hide behind it. It's understandable. They don't want to be hurt again by something they once either tried to believe in or saw someone else believe in and fail miserably.

In verse 5, Paul also explains what a stronghold is in a Biblical context. With the spiritual weapons that we've been given, we can pull down strongholds and cast down *"arguments and every high thing that exalts itself against the knowledge of God, bringing every thought into captivity to the obedience of Christ"* (2 Corinthians 10:5).

There are strongholds in every individual's life. Although, it is important to know that these strongholds always have a source and an author to them, they do not need to be over-spiritualized. It's not a demonic oppression or possession on someone's life. It's just a defense mechanism that we all have. Oftentimes, we use these strongholds to justify why we feel the need to do something or believe a certain way.

MY GOLDEN RULE

For example, the Bible does not say that drinking is a sin. Being drunk is a sin, but not drinking itself. However, I know many people (who might even be reading this) who have to hide behind a stronghold to defend why they can drink. They feel the need to justify it to everyone. My golden rule is that if I have to justify something in my life, I probably shouldn't be doing it. Even if it isn't necessarily wrong or sinful, if I need to justify and prove to everyone why it's okay, I'd be better off not doing it in the first place.

Think of it this way: I rarely hear anyone justifying why they go to church every Sunday, but I often hear people justifying why they just *have* to go on vacation on a Sunday and miss church. Usually their excuse is because they don't want to use vacation days or they're all out of vacation days. In reality, the value of attending church should outweigh the loss of a few dollars on our next paycheck, but I digress.

Another example: I don't hear people trying to justify heterosexual marriage. What I do hear is people trying to justify and make others accept same-sex marriage. When we know something is the right thing, there is rarely a need to try to justify it. Sometimes, people are just really self-conscious and need people's approval. This is why we need to stop operating in pride, as I mentioned earlier in this book.

Do you see what I'm saying? All of those things are just strongholds in people's lives, and we have been given the weapons to pull those strongholds down in our own lives and in the lives of others.So how do we do it?

> *And take the helmet of salvation, and the sword of the Spirit, which is the word of God.*
>
> **Ephesians 6:17**

OUR SPIRITUAL WEAPON

One of the weapons we have been given in our arsenal is the Sword of the Spirit, which is the Word of God. I told you that the Word is powerful! When we begin to renew our minds to God's Word, we are using that weapon to break down strongholds in our own minds.

In Ephesians 6, Paul talks about putting on the entire armor of God to protect ourselves from the attacks of the devil. However, if you've ever noticed, every single weapon it describes is used for defense except for the Word of God–the Sword of the Spirit. We only need one attacking weapon because this weapon is too powerful. The young kids today would say that this weapon is "O.P." or "overpowered."

Take a look at 2 Corinthians again, but this time in the New International Version:

> *We demolish arguments and every pretension that sets itself up against the knowledge of God, and we take captive every thought to make it obedient to Christ.*
>
> **2 Corinthians 10:5 (NIV)**

All of these strongholds and arguments that we break down go against what God's Word says. When someone tries to argue that healing passed away with the apostles or that sometimes God heals and sometimes He doesn't, that's an argument that completely goes against God's Word. And when you are diagnosed with an incurable disease, and your doctor tells you that you're going to die, that goes against what the Word of God says.

The way that we demolish and cast down these vain imaginations is by bringing all of those negative thoughts captive and making them submit to Jesus, the Word. You can't keep a bird from flying over your head, but you can keep it from making a nest in your hair. Likewise, we can't stop thoughts from coming, but we can tell them where to go. Whenever a negative thought tries to enter my mind, I confront it like Mike Wazowski from *Monsters Inc.* and say, "Put that thing back where it came from, or so help me!"

The way that we demolish and cast down these vain imaginations is by bringing all of those negative thoughts captive and making them submit to Jesus, the Word.

Just like in a war, after you conquer your enemy and bring all the captives to the captain, you need to ring every false thought before Jesus, our captain. For some of you, you might be dealing with more negative thoughts than others. That just means you have to work double time to put them in order, but over time, as you continue your walk in the Lord and begin to put the Word in your heart, these negative thoughts come less often. I can't promise you that they will never come back, but I can promise that you will have the weapons available to cast them down and overcome every evil thought.

CHAPTER 5 DISCUSSION:

1. How am I currently sowing the seed of God's Word in my life? What steps can I take to ensure it takes root and grows effectively?
2. In what areas of my life do I need to exercise patience and perseverance, trusting in God's timing and His promises? How can I strengthen my faith during these times?
3. What strongholds or defensive mental fortresses do I recognize in my own thinking or beliefs? How can I use the Word of God to break down these strongholds and align my thoughts more closely with Christ?
4. Reflecting on my own spiritual journey, where have I experienced God's faithfulness in waiting for His promises to be fulfilled? How can I encourage others who may be in a similar season of waiting?
5. In what ways can I more effectively use the Sword of the Spirit (God's Word) in my daily life to combat negative thoughts, doubts, or challenges to my faith? What practical steps can I take to renew my mind consistently with Scripture?

REFLECT ON WHAT THE HOLY SPIRIT SPOKE TO YOU IN THIS CHAPTER:

Chapter 6

Be On The Attack

My grandfather served and fought in the Vietnam War. Growing up, I would be spoiled by story after story about his times in battle. It's incredible to hear about his close encounters with enemy soldiers and how God protected him throughout his time there.

I've always had a fascination with the military. I would play war video games and watch war movies (and I still love those types of movies based on true events). However, one thing that I find interesting is how much war has evolved from the days of Jesus to modern times. One example of this evolution is in the way we fight and protect ourselves. Today, our soldiers are equipped with Interceptor Body Armor (IBA), a bullet-resistant plate carrier worn over their uniforms. With that, you'll find soldiers wearing a helmet on top.

Where did the shields and swords go? Back in Paul's day, that was the standard in battle! There were no guns or grenades, but they fought with swords, spears, and shields. In his letters to the Ephesians, Paul explains how we as Christians need to wear armor, just like the

Roman and Greek soldiers who went out to battle. However, our armor is not to protect us from physical weapons but spiritual ones.

We are in a spiritual battle, and failure to realize that doesn't mean the battle doesn't exist, it just means you'll lose the battle every time. And since we are in this spiritual battle, we need spiritual armor and spiritual weapons to render ourselves victorious. In 1 Samuel, the young shepherd boy David went out to challenge Goliath, the giant, because he was defying the children of God. When King Saul heard about David, he called him into his war tent and "clothed David with his armor" (1 Samuel 17:38). However, David tried to walk, but because the armor didn't fit him, he removed it entirely and fought Goliath without it.

That is the equivalent of us trying to fight these spiritual battles with physical weapons and armor. It won't work out for us. So, what armor can we use?

> *Put on the whole armor of God, that you may be able to stand against the wiles of the devil.*
>
> **Ephesians 6:11**

Paul tells us to put on God's own armor for ourselves. This armor consists of the **belt of truth**, the **breastplate of righteousness** (Ephesians 6:14), the **shoes of peace** (Ephesians 6:15), the **shield of faith** (Ephesians 6:16), the **helmet of salvation** and the **sword of the Spirit** (Ephesians 6:17). In these six items, every one of them is a defensive piece of armor except for the sword of the Spirit, "which is the Word of God" (Ephesians 6:17).

THE POWER OF GOD'S WORD

You'd think that there should be more than one attacking weapon in your arsenal but God's Word is so powerful, that's all you need.

> *For the word of God is living and powerful, and sharper than any two-edged sword, piercing even to the division of soul and spirit, and*

of joints and marrow, and is a discerner of the thoughts and intents of the heart.

Hebrews 4:12

God's Word is alive! It's sharper than any two-edged sword. The word "powerful" in the Greek is *energḗs*, which means "active, operative" (Strong's Concordance). The New International Version translates this verse as "For the word of God is living and active." This "sword" is so powerful and sharp that it is able to cut through the hardest of hearts. Regardless of the strongholds you have in your heart, God's Word is able and capable to pierce through it and tear down those walls.

HOW TO HEAR GOD'S VOICE

One of the things I often hear in ministry is people asking me, "How do I know if what I believe is from God or not?" After all, God will mostly speak to us through our hearts. Your heart is comprised of both the soul and the spirit (the soul being carnal and the spirit being spiritual). God will speak through your spirit, and that voice will be delivered to your mind. Hearing God isn't as complicated as most people think. We need to quiet our minds because God is always speaking to us in our spirit, but because our minds are chaotic, we have a hard time hearing Him.

To discern whether or not you're hearing from God in your heart is through His Word. God's Word is capable of "piercing even to the division of soul and spirit." Only under the intense scrutiny of God's Word can we discern what is spiritual and what is fleshly. A desire in your heart can sound great, but if it's not from God, it's not worth pursuing.

When you become single-minded with God's Word, it will be so much easier and effortless to discern the voice of God. With His Word as your attacking weapon, you can pierce through negative thoughts! It's exactly how I stayed in faith when I ate those bad chicken and dumplings. I used God's Word to stand on and fend off evil thoughts.

I believe Paul needed this revelation because he went through a lot of physical hardship and mental hardship. When you are on a mission to do what God calls you to do, and you end up getting shipwrecked, left for dead, beaten, whipped, and persecuted by religious and political leaders, it can take a toll on your mind. But this is exactly what these spiritual weapons and armor are designed for.

The shield of faith is not just a shield to protect you in the front but a shield that protects you from the back, too! The shield's job is to "quench all the fiery darts of the wicked one" (Ephesians 6:16). Paired with the sword of the Spirit, a soldier with this combination can be extremely deadly to the enemy.

If you have to 'get ready,' it's because you aren't ready.

These two complement each other. How do you remain in faith when your world seems to be crashing down? Paul said in Romans that "faith comes by hearing and hearing by the Word of God" (Romans 10:17). The Word of God is what you need when you feel your faith depleting. Every single one of those pieces of armor is essential if you want to experience total and complete victory in your walk with Christ.

THE BATTLE FOR YOUR MIND

The battle is not fought out in the physical world but in the spirit–more specifically, your mind. The enemy is constantly looking to find a weak spot in your armor. The only weapon that he possesses is the power of deception. If he can get you to believe a lie, he's won that battle.

The devil can't force you to do anything without your consent and cooperation. He didn't force Eve to eat the fruit in the Garden. He deceived her. Likewise, that is the same trick and tactic that he uses on us today. If we aren't prepared and equipped to fight the battle in our minds, we will lose.

I heard this preacher repeatedly tell his church to "Get ready, get ready, get ready," and his church loved it. But the Lord told me, "*If you have to 'get ready,' it's because you aren't ready.*" Preparation time is never wasted time, but there comes a point where you have to *be* ready.

Now the Spirit expressly says that in latter times some will depart from the faith, giving heed to deceiving spirits and doctrines of demons.

1 Timothy 4:1

This verse does not entirely infer that people will walk away from God. I'm sure some will, but this is more about believers making the conscious decision to stop believing the Apostles' doctrine. What were some of the teachings that the Apostles were in agreement on? Healing, prosperity, righteousness through Jesus and not through works, the resurrection of Jesus, the gifts of the Holy Spirit, and others not mentioned.

The phrase "will depart from" is the Greek verb *aphístēmi*. This Greek word means "cause to withdraw...to desert...to go away, depart" (Thayer's Greek-English Lexicon). These people who depart from the faith are the ones Jesus who had the Word sown in their hearts, but because of life experiences, they fall away or become offended (Mark 4:16-17). The reason they stop believing isn't because of the experience but because of deception through the experience.

I say that because, like others, I've been through a handful of afflictions in my mature Christian life, but I've stayed the course. I know great people of faith who have overcome terminal illnesses, serve God, and still believe it's His will to heal, while others get a cold and refuse to believe. It's not the experience or circumstances that make a person stop believing but the deception that comes with those circumstances.

No one in their right mind would depart from the goodness of God if it weren't for demonic deception in their life. "Giving heed" to these deceiving spirits means to devote thought and effort to" (Thayer's Greek-English Lexicon) and also "to hold the mind" (Strong's Concordance). It's important to know that in the Greek, this is a present-tense word, meaning that it is a continuous action and not something they once did.

GUARDING AGAINST DECEPTION

These deceptive spirits manipulate people's beliefs by attacking their thoughts with things like unforgiveness, "The church hurt me," "All Christians are hypocrites," "Jesus isn't the only way, all religions lead to God, "Homosexuality is not a sin," "God wants me sick," embracing scientific theories over biblical truth, believing false religions and many more.

Regardless of the deception, the end result is the same: distorting and misrepresenting the truth. According to the Spirit of God, these are all signs of the end times. Paul said that these things would occur in "latter times," which began nearly 2,000 years ago. If this was happening then it will only increase as we approach the Lord's Second Coming.

There are many ways that the devil will try to deceive you into believing a lie, but Jesus told us the main way in Mark 4.

> *And these are they likewise which are sown on stony ground; who, when they have heard the word, immediately receive it with gladness; And have no root in themselves, and so endure but for a time: afterward, when affliction or persecution ariseth for the word's sake, immediately they are offended.*
>
> **Mark 6:16-17 KJV**

Jesus said that the number one reason persecution and affliction come is for the Word's sake. Remember, the Word of God is the sword of the Spirit. If the devil can disarm you of your most effective attacking weapon and keep you on the defense, he will. You have to come to a place in your life where you will not be gullible and easy prey to the enemy and start standing on God's Word.

The word "offended" is the Greek word *skandalízō*. This is where we get the word "scandal." It can be translated as "to cause a person to begin to distrust and desert one whom he ought to trust and obey." The one person who you should trust and obey is God, and if the devil can get you to believe a lie about God, it will cause you to stop trusting in God.

EYES ON JESUS AMIDST FAILURES

Think about this for a moment. What usually happens when a leader of great influence commits a scandal? You stop trusting them.

Back in 2018, there was a huge scandal in one of America's largest churches. This pastor had started his church back in the 70's and built it into a megachurch. He had allegations made against him about having a prolonged affair with a married woman. This woman ended up retracting all of her allegations, but more people came forward, accusing the man of sexual misconduct decades prior. Because of these allegations, this pastor lost everything that he built. Not only that, his entire board of elders resigned, and no one wanted to step up and assume the role of the lead pastor. It was a disaster.

Since then, he has maintained a low profile and isn't in the ministry. This doesn't mean God can't use him, but it does mean that this man has lost credibility and trust from a lot of people. Whether the allegations were true or false, they still caused him to lose the important aspect of our relationships: trust.

Fix your gaze solely upon Jesus, 'the author and perfecter of our faith'

Remember this: The enemy will go to great lengths to sow doubt about God in your mind, even by exploiting the failings of humans. Idolizing pastors and leaders, putting them on a pedestal as if they were Jesus, can lead to problems that the devil can exploit. People are flawed, and when they make mistakes (as they inevitably will), the devil will try to persuade you that they are not to be trusted. This is why we must turn to the Word of God to counter such thoughts. Paul urges us to fix our gaze solely upon Jesus, "the author and perfecter of our faith" (Hebrews 12:2).

The Word of God serves as your spiritual weapon, capable of demolishing every stronghold in your mind. This is the essence of renewing your mind—letting go of negative thoughts and misconceptions about God, people, and life, and embracing the truth found in God's Word.

Sanctify them [purify, consecrate, separate them for Yourself, make them holy] by the Truth; Your Word is Truth.

John 17:17 AMPC

Remember this: The Word of God isn't just filled with truth; it is Truth. When you plant God's Word in your heart, you'll begin to see yourself through God's eyes. Every negative thought will have to yield to the truth you *know*. Jesus also said that it's the truth you *know* that sets you free (John 8:32).

If you don't know it, it won't change you. Knowing the truth is deeper than just reading or hearing about it. It's like a husband intimately knowing his wife. I know a lot about my wife Stephanie, but every day, I discover new things about her. The day I stop discovering new things about her is the day I stop seeking. Similarly, the day the Word of God becomes uninteresting is the day we stop valuing it.

CHAPTER 6 DISCUSSION:

1. Which piece of the spiritual armor do you feel you need to focus on strengthening in your own life?
2. Can you recall a time when you experienced a spiritual battle? How did you respond, and what could you have done differently using the truths you read in this chapter?
3. What steps can you take to deepen your understanding and application of the Bible in order to effectively use it as a spiritual weapon?
4. What challenges do you face in discerning God's voice amid the chaos of daily life?
5. How do you stay vigilant against deception, and what practices can help you remain grounded in the truth of God's Word?

REFLECT ON WHAT THE HOLY SPIRIT SPOKE TO YOU IN THIS CHAPTER:

Chapter 7

Understanding God's Nature

Do you know how to distinguish between a genuine bill and a counterfeit one? Some people hold the bill up to the light or use a special marker, but do you know the most reliable method to determine its authenticity?

The U.S. Secret Service, which is tasked with safeguarding the country's financial system, stresses the importance of familiarizing yourself with the security features of authentic currency. They provide resources and training materials that focus on understanding the specific traits of real bills.

Additionally, the Federal Reserve Bank offers educational materials that encourage the examination of genuine currency characteristics to spot counterfeits. They stress the significance of learning the distinct features of real currency, including watermarks, security threads, and color-shifting ink.

One of the best ways to spot a fake is to be well-acquainted with the real deal. My dad, grandpa, and I have a habit of playing pranks on each other over the phone. For instance, when I'm with my dad and my grandpa calls him, I'll answer the phone pretending to be my dad. Other times, when I try to call my grandpa, my dad will pick up and pretend to be him. It's all fun until I catch onto a few words that sound unlike my grandpa. I'm familiar with my grandpa's mannerisms and habits, so when something seems off, I can tell it's not really him.

DESTROYING WRONG THINKING

Now, why am I even bringing all of this up? There are many false narratives about God, His character, and His Word that too many people are falling prey to simply because they don't know God's real nature. Back in 2020, the world was hit with a pandemic called COVID-19. It seemed as if everyone was on the same page that God sent COVID to get the world to repent, specifically the USA). They instilled fear into so many people across our nation because they had a wrong mentality about God's nature.

In the process of learning to control our thoughts and live more mindfully, we need to destroy wrong thinking. So far, throughout this book, we've been identifying some truths in God's Word about who we are in Him and who He is in us. In the previous chapters, we discussed what it looks like to pull down strongholds and cast down vain imaginations, and now we need to apply these things in our lives.

Believe it or not, many people have a wrong mindset regarding God. They tend to think of Him as more of the Godfather instead of God the Father. These people know that God loves them and has a plan for their lives, but they have a misunderstanding of that love and His true nature. So now, we need to identify some false narratives about Him by studying His true, authentic nature.

> *Nor do they put new wine into old wineskins, or else the wineskins break, the wine is spilled, and the wineskins are ruined. But they put new wine into new wineskins, and both are preserved.*
>
> **Matthew 9:17 KJV**

CHANGE OUT THE OLD WINESKIN

You can't have a new way of thinking without first discarding your old way of thinking. In this example, Jesus was using the illustration of wineskins. The wineskins used in His day were the leather of an animal–usually a goat. People would place new wine inside of these new wineskins and let the wine ferment over time. During the fermentation, the wineskins would begin to expand and stretch until the wine was ready for drinking.

Once the wine was removed from the wineskin, it would be discarded and not used again. This is because the wineskin would become brittle and delicate. If someone were to use that old, used-up wineskin with new wine, the old wineskin would burst and ruin both the new wine and the old wineskin. That wouldn't be good.

New wine needs new wineskins, and new understanding needs a renewed mind.

With this illustration in mind, we can relate the new wine to the New Covenant we have with God, and the wineskin is the way we think and our mindset. If you never grew up in church, chances are, you don't have an old wineskin that needs to be discarded. The old wineskin can refer to an Old Covenant mindset we have about God. Many people have an Old Covenant understanding of God and His nature when Jesus has been trying to give them new wine. They can't receive this new wine or this new understanding unless they discard their old mindset and have a new mindset. I like to say it like this: new wine needs new wineskins, and new understanding needs a renewed mind.

Jesus gave us too much grace and truth through His sacrifice on the cross for the Old Covenant to contain. The Old Covenant says, "Do this, and God will bless you," while the New Covenant says, "God has blessed you, so go and do this." Some people can't tell the difference in that statement. Trust me, it's not just semantics.

The difference is the former deals with a conditional relationship with God. Have you ever heard the phrase, "You scratch my back, and I'll scratch yours?" That was the Old Covenant. If we listened and obeyed the Law, blessings would be a reward.

The latter statement deals with an unconditional relationship with God. God has empowered us because of what Jesus did on the cross. Because we have been blessed with every spiritual blessing in heavenly places, we can now follow His commands guilt-free!

It's imperative that you understand this because you cannot receive all that God has for you with an old mindset. You'll end up spoiling the new wine. In the Old Covenant, God would deal with mankind according to their goodness–or lack of it. If they failed to uphold the law in its entirety, God would deal with them accordingly. This wasn't because God was mean and liked to inflict punishment on His kids, but because He is a just and holy God, He couldn't let sin be unpunished. Someone had to be accountable for their sins.

You cannot receive all that God has for you with an old mindset.

When Jesus died on the cross, He took the responsibility for mankind's past, present, and even future sins (sins you haven't even committed yet) and took our place in the wrath of God. God has already dealt with mankind's failure to uphold the law perfectly when He sacrificed His Son. When Jesus said, "It is finished," in John 19:30, He was referring to the works of the Law being fulfilled. He didn't just take our place on the cross, but He actually upheld the Law in its entirety. That was the only way to fulfill the Law and extinguish the wrath of God.

Unfortunately, many people have made the work of Jesus vain in their lives (1 Corinthians 1:17). How do they do that? By continuing to relate to God through an Old Covenant mindset.

BORN AGAIN AGAIN?

You might have been operating with an Old Covenant mindset without even knowing it! Before the Lord turned me on to these amazing truths, I know that I was. I remember being in youth group and going up to the altar week after week because I had sinned and messed up since the last youth service. Each week, the youth pastor would give us a message and, at the end, give us time to come to the altar and "rededicate" our lives to Christ. Even on Sunday morning during "big church," I heard the pastor give the adults the same opportunity; only in this setting would he invite those who have "backslid" against the Lord.

In either instance, they would make us feel really bad about sinning and falling short and guilt us without actually guilting us, which I think is the term "gaslighting." Each week, I would feel terrible for not living up to God's standards and then come forward to the altar and say the same prayer: "Dear Jesus, I'm sorry for my sins. Please forgive me. Wash me. Cleanse me. I give my life to you. Amen."

There are many things wrong with that prayer. And sadly, it's being taught by pastors all over the world. Every time I sinned, I thought I was going to hell unless I confessed my sins and asked for forgiveness. In a way, I was taught that unless I put my sins under the blood, I was going to hell. If that were true, the best chance of you getting to heaven after I led you through that prayer is if I shoot you after you said, "Amen."

Every week, I rededicated my life to Christ and became born again, again. Then, the next week, I would do it all over again and become born again, again, again...And the next week...You know where this is going.

I was born again to the 12th power! If there were such things as super saints, I would be the greatest super saint with how many times I got born again. The truth that no one told me was that once I got born again the very first time, it was a done deal for all of eternity. God loved me so much that it didn't matter what I had done against Him. Nothing could ever separate me from my Father's love (Romans 8:38).

RESTORATION BY REVELATION

I didn't get a hold of this revelation until 2017. My entire Christian life before that, I felt like a worm—never good enough in God's eyes, having made too many mistakes for God to use someone like me. I never drank in high school, smoked weed, or did any of that in spite of my entire friend group doing those things. I lived a relatively better life than all of my friends in church, yet I still felt unworthy.

God loved me so much that it didn't matter what I had done.

One of my biggest regrets in life was losing my virginity at the age of 14. I had never had a real girlfriend until that point in my life. My first kiss was in the 8th grade when I was 13, and right after my freshmen year of high school began, I was introduced to my first girlfriend. I really don't regret many things in my life, but this one is something I always dealt with.

After my first relationship, I entered into a few more, falling for the same stupid stuff. It was a cycle of bad decisions. Throughout the week, I served in our youth group on the worship team! Every single Wednesday night, I would feel so guilty, condemned, and unworthy for what I had done the day before I got on stage (and sometimes hours before). Guilt is a good trigger emotion to tell you that what you're doing is wrong and to stop, but lingering guilt and condemnation are never from God. That's what I was living in–lingering guilt.

In fact, what made that guilt and condemnation worse was when one of my pastors (someone I looked up to greatly) told me that when the day that I get married to my wife comes, every woman that I've ever slept with will be standing behind her. The amount of guilt and pressure that I felt because of wrong teaching made me hide things from my wife! It's like when Adam and Eve ate the fruit of the Tree of Knowledge of Good and Evil. Immediately after they ate it, they hid from God. The reason why they hid was because they were afraid (Genesis 3:10).

God's grace has been so imminent in my life that my wife and I can look back and laugh about this, but when we were just friends back in 2014, I knew that she hadn't been with a man and was saving herself for her future husband (which would be me, she just didn't want to accept it at the time). One day, we were texting, asking some personal questions that I admittedly initiated, and the question came up for me to answer if I was a virgin or not. At this point, I definitely was not. But because of fear of what Stephanie might think about me if she knew the truth, I lied and told her that I still had my V-card. At the time, I thought, *It's just a little white lie. She'll never know anyway.* Wait...did you hear that? Oh, never mind. It's just the sound of my lie backfiring on me years later!

I lied because, just like Adam and Eve, I was afraid and insecure. I was afraid because I had never received God's love and grace in this area in the first place, and I thought Stephanie was going to judge me, too. I didn't know that God had already forgiven me and that I could live a guilt-free life with Him, so why would a person give me that grace? Lying wasn't the only issue that arose from not knowing this.

Have you ever been on a diet and made good progress until suddenly you cave and eat a big fat slice of chocolate cake? Then, after you eat that slice, you think, *Well, I already caved. One more slice won't hurt* until, eventually, you've eaten the whole thing. That's essentially what I did. I continued in a sexually immoral lifestyle throughout high school. I had thought that since I was already impure to God, why stop?

After the relationship I had before Stephanie ended, I started taking my relationship with God more seriously. I wasn't seeing anyone, and Stephanie and I began talking again after not speaking for over a year (because of my last relationship). At this point, it's been years since I had told her the little white lie. Our friendship picked up where we last left it and we have talked every single day since then. We would go get lunch together and hang out with friends until things started getting more serious. We knew that this was leading to something more. One of Stephanie's mentors (who happened to know my ex) had told Stephanie some...things.

Needless to say, she found out that I was, in fact, *not* a virgin, and she felt betrayed and lied to. Rightfully so. She didn't address this right away, and we ended up not speaking to each other for a few weeks until she had sorted out her thoughts and feelings. To continue with this honesty streak, I was head-over-heels in love with Stephanie at this point and was so worried about why she wanted some space after it seemed like everything was going so smoothly.

Leading up to all of this, I had received God's love and forgiveness in this area and was now confident in Him. I had been restored in my heart, and I knew that God could renew my sexuality. Weeks later, she ended up confronting me about it during a 2-mile walk around her neighborhood! Great timing, Stephanie. Way to trap me!

During that conversation, she asked me why I had lied to her all those years ago. She was walking into this relationship with the full expectation that I had saved myself for my future wife, and now she has just found out the opposite. I apologized for lying to her and accepted the reality that she might never want to be in a relationship with me. A guy who lost it to some girl six years ago. However, now, I have been restored in my heart by God, and I told her, "I know that God has forgiven me, and I have forgiven myself." This was my way of saying, "If you have an issue with it, that's on you!"

I manned up and admitted my wrongdoing, but I also didn't waiver in my confidence in God's grace in my life. Before this point, I wouldn't have been able to say that. Prior, I didn't know what I deserved, but God did.

Stephanie is the grace of God in my life. At one of my lowest points in life, God gave me Stephanie. Someone who didn't care about my past but cared more about why I felt the need to lie. Even when she saved herself for her future husband, and I hadn't done that for her, she still chose to love me. With knowledge of my sexual history in relationships, one of my other mentors told me, "You should take a complete year off of dating before you enter into a relationship with Stephanie." I did not listen. I didn't listen because now, in that season of my life, I have had a revelation of my identity in Christ. I knew that if I was in Christ, I was a new creation, and old things have passed away and all things have become new (2 Corinthians 5:17). I was confident that I could do this without messing up again.

My old mentality was keeping me away from what God really had for me.

Needless to say, we got past that issue and started dating later that year. After a year of dating, I was proud to admit that we refrained from having sex, and I went back to that mentor and told him. He was shocked. So was I! I was shocked that I actually did it, but I wasn't shocked in God's grace. Another year of dating without having sex followed before I got on one knee and proposed to Stephanie, and after a six-month-long engagement, we tied the knot in 2019.

I was able to protect our relationship the best way that I could because I had a new understanding and revelation of what God thought about me. I had to change my thinking completely. My old mentality was keeping me away from what God really had for me. It didn't matter what things I had done in the past; God could restore me. If you are boggled down with the weight of guilt and condemnation, I want you to know that God can and will restore you, no matter what you've done in the past. You just need to change your wineskin.

DON'T DO AS THE ROMANS DO

Have you ever heard the phrase, "What you don't know can't hurt you?" What I've come to find out is that what you don't know can actually kill you in the long run. Some people like to ignore certain issues in their lives or hide them in a junk closet and pretend that they simply don't exist. Denying the truth doesn't diminish its validity. All it does is keep you from benefiting from the truth.

During the Roman Empire, people in positions of leadership and high-born Romans used to drink their beverages from cups and gauntlets. Little did they know that most of those vessels contained high traces of lead. They even ignorantly used lead pipes to channel water from the springs into their homes. Over time, these leaders and high-born Romans developed all sorts of health issues related to lead poisoning. What they didn't know literally killed them.

My people are destroyed for lack of knowledge.

Hosea 4:6 KJV

In Hosea, this was the Lord speaking through the prophet Hosea. The people were acting in such a lawless manner that it was literally destroying them. In its context, they didn't know that what they were doing was hurting them in the long run, so the Lord gave them this word. They didn't know about the negative effects that their actions were causing on them. This can also be applied to us when we don't know about the positive things God wants to give to us through His Word.

It is only through the correct knowledge of God that we can experience His goodness. In fact, "all things that pertain unto life and godliness" only come to us through the knowledge of Him (2 Peter 1:3). So it's safe to say that if you do not know God's Word, you will not know what He wants to give to you in this life. There are blessings that are waiting for you to receive on this side of eternity. I would hate to get to heaven at the end of my life and see all of the blessings that I missed out on while I was on the earth because of ignorance.

If you have grown up with a mindset that God doesn't want you to prosper or that God doesn't want you healed, the way you get rid of that demonic deception is solely through knowledge of His Word. The Amplified Bible translation says, "For His divine power has bestowed on us [absolutely] everything necessary for [a dynamic spiritual] life and godliness, **through true and personal knowledge of Him** who called us by His own glory and excellence." This mindset shift comes through a personal knowledge of our Good Father.

Just like how I received restoration through a new mentality about God, you can, too. You don't have to stay stuck in guilt and shame. You don't need to suffer from your sickness anymore. Jesus has purchased your healing. He has redeemed you from your sins, and He remembers them no more (Hebrews 8:12). Jesus said that it is only through the truth that you know that will set you free (John 8:32). That is what I am sharing with you today; the truth that has the potential to set you free. All you need to do with this truth is know it personally. Remove every other mindset you've had about God, plant this into your heart, and watch our amazing God heal you from the inside out.

CHAPTER 7 DISCUSSION:

1. How does the chapter challenge your perception of God's character and nature, particularly in contrast to common misconceptions?
2. What are some prevalent false narratives about God that the chapter addresses? How do these impact people's beliefs and behaviors?
3. According to the chapter, why is it crucial to renew your mind and discard old ways of thinking? How does this concept relate to personal growth and spiritual maturity?
4. Reflecting on the analogy of new wine in new wineskins, how can you apply this principle practically in your life to experience greater spiritual freedom and growth?
5. How does Hosea 4:6 resonate with the themes discussed in the chapter? What role does knowledge of God's Word play in experiencing His blessings and overcoming false beliefs?

REFLECT ON WHAT THE HOLY SPIRIT SPOKE TO YOU IN THIS CHAPTER:

Chapter 8

God Didn't Do It!

Have you ever asked the question, "Why do bad things happen to good people?" I remember being in high school and wondering the same thing. I would see terrible events on the news and ask my parents and pastors why there was so much bad in the world. It seemed like no matter who you were or what you've done, bad things happened.

I had a great boss in my life when I just finished high school. For the sake of his privacy, I'll call him Hugh. Hugh was known all throughout the area where I live. Everyone knew his name. He had built a great business and was very successful in the eyes of many. On top of his success, he was the nicest, most generous person you could ever meet. Any chance that he would get to help those in need, Hugh would jump all over it. I remember going with him to buy all the turkeys in one grocery store and then buying pumpkin pies from Costco to give to people for free during Thanksgiving week. Hugh was awesome.

One day, I got the very sad and awful news that Hugh had gone on to be with the Lord. Unfortunately, he ended his life prematurely. I remember being in an Airbnb in Roseville, California when I got wind of the news. I hadn't seen or spoken to him since I left the job I was employed under him years before. Regardless, I was completely shocked. What shocked me the most was that he was such a happy and nice person.

WHY DID GOD ALLOW IT?

During the next few days, I processed what had happened and tried to make sense of it. I remember asking God, "Why didn't you stop this?" I was sincerely confused and frustrated as to why God allowed this to happen. The thought that God let this awesome guy, who has done great things for the Lord and so many people, end his own life left me spiraling. I didn't get an answer until years later. Not because God wasn't speaking to me but because I wasn't listening.

After years of seeking the Lord and finding out the true nature of God, I was shown Mark chapter 4. I touched on this briefly in Chapter 6, *Be On The Attack*, and I want to dive in a little deeper with you.

> *These likewise are the ones sown on stony ground who, when they hear the word, immediately receive it with gladness; and they have no root in themselves, and so endure only for a time. Afterward, when tribulation or persecution arises for the word's sake, immediately they stumble.*
>
> **Mark 4:16-17**

Jesus said that persecution and affliction come for one reason only: to steal God's Word out of your heart. Remember that the word "affliction" can be defined as "burden, pressure, or trouble" in your life. This qualifies anything that is a burden or that causes unwanted stress in your life as coming from the devil and not from God.

The enemy is always trying to get you to stop trusting in God by doubting His character. He does this by using hardships like this in life. This circumstance caused me to question God in an area that I had thought I was secure in. It usually isn't until your boat gets rocked that you find out if you have your sea legs or not. I was rocked. I didn't question if God was good or not, but I questioned why He failed to intervene. All-powerful, all-knowing God could do anything but did do nothing? Something was wrong in my theology.

The enemy is always trying to get you to stop trusting in God by doubting His character.

The parable of the sower in Mark 4 is the most important parable for us to understand. In fact, Jesus said that if we didn't understand this one, then we couldn't understand any of the parables that He taught (Mark 4:13) because this parable deals with the conditions of the heart. The stony ground (which is the ground Jesus is talking about) is the people who hear God's Word, love it and receive it, but they don't have a commitment to studying God's Word more. They are shallow Christians or "Carnal Christians." They aren't able to withstand the hardships of life because their roots are shallow. The understanding of God and His nature is far short of what it should be.

These hardships come to wipe out the devil's competition. The devil is trying to sift the body of Christ like wheat to find the weak Christians (Luke 22:31). He is walking about "as a roaring lion seeking whom he may devour" (1 Peter 5:8). He will use the death of a loved one, a lingering sickness, an intrusive thought, just to get you to doubt what you thought you knew about God. I go into more detail about this topic in my teaching, *Is God Out To Get Me?*

SAME GIFT, DIFFERENT BOX

The scary reality of this is that it works really well. This tactic that the enemy likes to use is very effective, and if it ain't broke, don't fix it. He's been doing this since the days of Adam and Eve and will continue to do this until he's cast down into the lake of fire forever. Once you find out that the devil's tactics are the same gift, just wrapped up in a different box, nothing should surprise you anymore.

> *He will not be afraid of evil tidings; His heart is steadfast, trusting in the Lord.*
>
> Psalm 112:7

This psalm is about the righteous person—that's you and me! It says that it doesn't matter what news comes our way or what issues pop up in our lives. We can be steadfast in the Lord and fear nothing! How do we get that to happen? I'll share with you how I did.

When I received bad news, my heart would race, my palms would sweat, and I would get nervous to my stomach. I was not responding like a righteous person. As Andrew Wommack says, I would fall apart like a two-dollar suitcase.

On the night of Jesus' crucifixion, He told His disciples many troubling things about the events that were soon to come concerning His death, burial, and resurrection and then proceeded to tell them to "be of good cheer; I have overcome the world" (John 16:33).

> *These things I have spoken to you, that in Me you may have peace. In the world you will have tribulation; but be of good cheer, I have overcome the world.*
>
> **John 16:33**

The word "tribulation" in John 16 is the same Greek word as "affliction" in Mark 4. Jesus practically promised us that we would have tribulation. However, Jesus did *not* say that He was the one sending the tribulation, which is what too many Christians fail to understand. I once heard my good friend Arthur Meintjes explain this concept, which I'll paraphrase: People like to blame God for the circumstances simply because God is always there at the scene of the incident. That's like blaming the paramedics for every automobile accident simply because they always happen to show up at the scene of the crash. The paramedics are there to *help*. Likewise, just because God is always there doesn't mean He caused it. He shows up to help you.

GUILTY BY ASSOCIATION

The first thing that I had to uproot from my stinkin' thinkin' was that God was the author of hardship in life. Going back to Hugh, I didn't necessarily believe God authored his passing, but I believed He allowed it. I asked Him, "Why didn't you stop this? Why did you let him die?" I was blaming God for what had happened.

If someone is trying to hurt my wife physically and I step aside and hand them the weapons, I would be just as guilty as the person who assaulted her. I might not have physically touched her myself, but I was involved. When we think God "allows" hardships in our lives, that is equivalent to that example. He would be guilty by association.

The issue with this has many dimensions. One problem that can occur with this mindset is that you blame God for something He had nothing to do with. Another problem that will manifest in your life is that you will stop trusting Him subconsciously.

Think about it: Why would you trust that God is good if you believe He is the one who needed your loved one in heaven more than you needed them on earth? Why would you believe that God wants you healed and whole if you believe He put that sickness on you in the first place? You might say you trust that He is good, but subconsciously, you don't. Our mind wants to prioritize things that logically make sense over things that don't make logical sense. And, logically speaking, if you think God kills people, then there is no way you can fully trust Him with your life. It is impossible.

Before you get so worked up about *why* bad things are happening, you have to understand one of the most important aspects: **God is not the source of it**. I want you to promise yourself, from this point on, that you will never again blame God for something bad that has happened in your life or in the lives of people around you. Let's look at an example in the Bible concerning this.

THE THORN IN THE FLESH

The Apostle Paul was one of, if not the greatest, of the Apostles. He received more revelation about God's character than anyone else. He wrote more than half of the New Testament from this revelation and inspiration from the Holy Spirit, and he suffered more than anyone else due to preaching the true Gospel.

> *And lest I should be exalted above measure by the abundance of the revelations, a thorn in the flesh was given to me, a messenger of Satan to buffet me, lest I be exalted above measure.*
>
> **2 Corinthians 12:7**

The "thorn in the flesh" has been long debated by scholars and TikTok influencers alike. Most people associate it with some sort of physical ailment that Paul dealt with in his later years. Some say he had poor eyesight, and others say he went mentally crazy. But all of those opinions and theories lack scriptural backing.

Paul was kidnapped (Acts 21:27), beaten (Acts 21:30-31; 23:3), threatened (Acts 22:22; 27:42), arrested many times (Acts 21:33; 22:24, 31; 23:35; 28:16), accused in lawsuits (Acts 21:34; 22:30; 24:1-2; 25:2, 7; 28:4), interrogated (Acts 25:24-27), ridiculed (Acts 26:24), ignored (Acts 27:11), shipwrecked (Acts 27:41) and bitten by a viper (Acts 28:3) and not to mention endured freezing conditions, hunger and starvation. If anyone knew hardship, it was Paul.

Paul stated here that because of the "abundance of revelations," he was given a thorn in the flesh, which he then defines as "a messenger of Satan," to keep him from becoming exalted above measure. Because Paul mentions that this was given to him so that he wouldn't be exalted "above measure," people assume that this affliction came from God to keep him humble. The issue with this idea is that the Bible speaks clearly about godly exalting and how it has nothing to do with pride. There are many examples of this, including God exalting Joshua so that the Israelites would follow his leadership.

All who desire to live godly in Christ Jesus will suffer persecution.

The issue here was that Paul was exalted and honored so much by people the devil tried to deflate his influence. Again, why did Jesus say affliction and persecution come for? The Word's sake. The devil will always try to make the Gospel unattractive because in it contains life-changing power. The way he did that in Paul's life was through persecution. Even in his letters to Timothy (his mentee), Paul warned him that "all who desire to live godly in Christ Jesus will suffer persecution" (2 Timothy 3:12).

Paul asks God to remove this thorn from him three times, but God says that His grace is sufficient for him. God didn't remove this thorn because we aren't redeemed from persecution in this life. People have a free will to do what they please. Hugh had a free will to do what he ended up doing, and (this might offend you) not even God could stop him from doing it. If you can understand this, you will withstand really hard circumstances in the future.

FREE WILL ISN'T ALWAYS FREE

Bad things happen to good people and bad people alike, and the reason for this is really simple. Free will. It's so simple that you need a good theologian to help you misunderstand it. Maybe you know someone who died in a car accident due to someone drinking and driving and thought, "Why did God allow this?" I want to help you understand the answer to that question I once had. God didn't allow it. Not in a million years did God want that to happen to your loved one.

There are a lot of things God doesn't want happening that are happening.

The Bible says that God doesn't will for anyone to perish–go to hell–but for all to come to repentance (2 Peter 3:9). The sad reality is that a lot of people are leaving this earth without Jesus every day. People have the free will to do what they want to do. There are a lot of things God doesn't want happening that are happening. The drunk driver of that car chose to be wreckless and get behind the wheel, and unfortunate events took place after.

God doesn't want anyone to go through any kind of sexual trauma, but because of the free will of people who are sick in the mind, traumatic events happen. I don't want to diminish the fact that whatever circumstances you have experienced are horrible things, but my aim is to help you understand that God isn't responsible.

What about sicknesses? Surely, someone doesn't have free will concerning that, right? You'd be surprised to find out that we have more of a say when it comes to sickness in our bodies staying or lingering. And because many Christians don't know or believe this, they are allowing sickness to stay in their bodies longer than necessary.

Then God said, Let Us make man in Our image, according to Our likeness; let them have dominion over the fish of the sea, over the birds of the air, and over the cattle, over all the earth and over every creeping thing that creeps on the earth.

Genesis 1:26

God has given all of us the authority and the dominion to rule this earth. Our life is our own responsibility. Our bodies are ours to control. Written all throughout the Bible are promises for us concerning life and health to our bodies. If we aren't planting those words in our hearts, we will not see the benefits of it.

And these signs will follow those who believe: In My name they will cast out demons; they will speak with new tongues; they will take up serpents; and if they drink anything deadly, it will by no means hurt them; they will lay hands on the sick, and they will recover.

Mark 16:17-18

These are the last words of Jesus before His ascension into Heaven. It says that these signs will follow only those who believe and one of those signs is that they will lay hands on the sick, and they *will* recover. It doesn't say that they might recover if you just pray hard enough. It says that they *will*. It's a promise. This isn't because of your power alone but because of the Holy Spirit living on the inside of you. The same spirit that raised Jesus from the dead lives in you and will bring to life your physical body, too (Romans 8:11).

God would no more put a sickness on one of His children than He would force someone to commit adultery. Since day one of Creation, the devil has been trying to get mankind to question their true authority and identity in Christ. He deceived Eve into believing that God was holding out on their full potential.

Satan will also try to deceive you into thinking wrongly about who you are in Christ. That's why we must resist the devil or actively fight against the devil, and he will flee from us (James 4:7). I bet that you have never heard this before, but you don't have to remain sick. You can be healed from whatever it is you are facing. Literally *whatever*.

You don't need to go to every doctor or psychiatrist to receive healing. You need Jesus. You need an understanding of God's true nature. You need to uproot wrong thinking.

Bad things aren't happening to you because you are a bad person or a good person. Bad things happen to us because of the devil. Whatever way he can steal the Word of God out of your heart, he will. If it takes getting you sick and accepting it, then he'll use that area. If it's getting you distracted by the love of money, he'll use that too. If it's causing a person to die a premature death to get you into doubt and unbelief, he will use that, too. That is why we need to uproot wrong thinking that believes God is the one doing these things and understand the true author of hardship–the devil.

The only reason why God would send hardship in your life is to teach you a lesson, which many people believe. However, here is how I know that God isn't punishing you based on your behavior:

> *For God so loved the world that He gave His only begotten Son, that whoever believes in Him should not perish but have everlasting life. For God did not send His Son into the world to condemn the world, but that the world through Him might be saved. He who believes in Him is not condemned; but he who does not believe is condemned already, because he has not believed in the name of the only begotten Son of God.*
>
> **John 3:16-18**

Jesus completely took the punishment and wrath of God so that we could be innocent in God's eyes (2 Corinthians 5:21 & Romans 10:4). God loved us so much that He sacrificed His only Son to die and take our place on that cross. The word "condemn" means to make someone guilty. The fact that God did not send Jesus to condemn us but to give us life is all the proof that we need to believe God is a good God and that He will never inflict hardship on us. We can truly start trusting in His goodness when this is understood in our hearts.

Everything Jesus did on earth was a direct representation of the heart of the Father (John 5:19). Jesus only did what He saw God do. Jesus never made someone sick or suffer to teach them a lesson. And He never refused to heal someone, either. Jesus only went around doing good, healing all those who the devil oppressed (Acts 10:38). Whatever he did on this earth was God's heart revealed to us.

> *The Spirit of the Lord is upon Me, Because He has anointed Me To preach the gospel to the poor; He has sent Me to heal the brokenhearted, To proclaim liberty to the captives And recovery of sight to the blind, To set at liberty those who are oppressed; To proclaim the acceptable year of the Lord.*
>
> **Luke 4:18-19**

His whole mission was to heal us and restore us. To reunite us with the Father once again. The very first message that Jesus preached about was about healing and favor. Once I understood this, it was like the scales fell off of my eyes, and I could see everything more clearly. I could see things for how they truly were.

TRUSTING IN THE LORD

Hardship doesn't shake me anymore. I don't fear when bad news comes. A few years ago, Stephanie and I were dealt bad news after bad news, but we were rock solid and unwavering in our faith as a family. The only reason why we were able to remain steadfast is because we trusted in God, just like it says in Psalm 112.

In the same conversation that Jesus had with the disciples in John chapter 16 about not being troubled because of tribulation, He started it by saying, "These things have I spoken unto you, that ye should not be **offended**" (John 16:1 KJV). Comparing that with what He said in verse 33, if we can keep our peace, we can keep ourselves from being offended.

> *You will keep him in perfect peace, whose mind is stayed on You, because he trusts in You.*
>
> **Isaiah 26:3**

I will touch on this more in the next chapter, but your peace is solely dependent on the amount that you trust in Jesus. Trust is formed by the way you think about someone. The more you are mindful of His goodness in your life, the more you can trust Him, and the more you will experience supernatural peace in the midst of bad circumstances.

Your mindset about God's nature can either save you or kill you. If you think God is the author of all of your life's issues, we serve two different gods. My God would never do that. My God wants to give us life and life more abundantly (John 10:10). My God sent Jesus to destroy the works of the devil (1 John 3:8). My God wants the best for me and my family (Jeremiah 29:11). Only until you embrace the true nature of God and understand His heart for you will you be able to break free from the questions and doubts you have in your mind. I did it. You can, too.

God wants to give us life and life more abundantly.

CHAPTER 8 DISCUSSION:

1. How have you personally grappled with the question, "Why do bad things happen to good people?" and what conclusions have you drawn from your experiences and faith?
2. Reflect on a time when you faced a significant hardship. How did it impact your faith and understanding of God's nature?
3. Understanding God's true nature is crucial for maintaining peace during tribulation. How do you personally cultivate and maintain this understanding?
4. How does free will shape your perspective on suffering and God's role in the hardships of life?
5. How can the parable of the sower in Mark 4 help us understand the reasons behind our spiritual struggles and tribulations?
6. Trust in God is formed by the way you think about Him. What practices or habits help you keep your mind focused on God's goodness, and how do these practices influence your peace during difficult times?

REFLECT ON WHAT THE HOLY SPIRIT SPOKE TO YOU IN THIS CHAPTER:

Chapter 9

Positioned for Peace

Let's familiarize ourselves with how we started this conversation in the first place. As Proverbs 23:7 says, our life is going in the exact direction of our dominant thought. The way that we think, how we view the world, and our dominant thoughts determine the direction that our lives will take. Having a negative mindset about God will lead to negative results while having a true understanding of God's nature will lead us to life and peace.

It takes true responsibility to realize that you are in control of the direction your life goes. The Bible doesn't tell us that "as a godly or wicked man thinks in his heart." It just says that as a man or a person. If you have a heartbeat and breath in your lungs, then you're qualified for this principle.

One major mindset you can have that will impact your life greatly is knowing how to have peace in the midst of chaotic or unfavorable circumstances. The reality of life is that we cannot control most circumstances that happen to us. Society tells us that we are the way that we are because we are simply products of our own environments. And, if you are a nervous wreck, it's because of your upbringing.

The world tells us that we cannot be anything other than how we were brought up. To a point, that is true. If you are solely in the world, then yes, I would have to agree with that. If you rely only on your own strength to experience life and peace, then you are only as good as how you were brought up. But, if you are in Jesus Christ, anything is possible. You can be free from anxiety and stress regardless of what circumstances come your way. You don't need to rely on Xanax or any other prescribed method to deal with stress. You can be at peace. Read that again. **You can be at peace.**

> *These things I have spoken to you while being present with you. But the Helper, the Holy Spirit, whom the Father will send in My name, He will teach you all things, and bring to your remembrance all things that I said to you. Peace I leave with you, My peace I give to you; not as the world gives do I give to you. Let not your heart be troubled, neither let it be afraid.*
>
> **John 14:25-27**

Jesus left us His peace. The peace of God that Jesus possessed while performing miracles is the same peace that He left for you and me to have. It's not a similar peace, but the exact same one.

A GIFT BEYOND MEASURE

I have a great friend in my life who I've looked up to and admired for some years. He and his wife started a church not too long before we did. For years, we could only admire them from a distance and through watching their online services, but the Lord opened a door in my life that allowed us to form a friendship.

One day, I was out playing pickleball with my dad for a good chunk of a winter morning. I hadn't checked my phone that entire time, and when I grabbed it, I saw that my friend had texted me out of the blue. It's always nice to receive a text from a friend out of nowhere, so I was already in a good mood because of it. But then I started reading the text, and he said, "Hey Matthew, do you know what size suit you wear?"

A million possibilities ran through my head. Is he going to buy me a new suit? Well, that was the only thought that ran through my head, I guess. We finished the conversation, and he decided to donate a few suits to me for the ministry. I was so blessed by it. But that's not even the best part. This was back in November, and at the beginning of each year, we have Big Vision Sunday at the church. I was getting my message ready and preparing for what God wanted to share with the church concerning 2024.

I was watching a few of their church services in the meantime and saw a specific jacket that he wore during a service. While I was watching it, I thought, "Man, I really hope that jacket is included in the ones he's giving to me." A few days pass before I get the package in the mail. After I got it, I opened it up and rifled through *all* of the things he sent. It wasn't just a few, like he said. It was a bunch.

Jesus has given us His peace. The exact one that He used and had Himself.

After I had just about finished going through all of them, I got the very last one at the bottom of the box, and there it was. *The* jacket. It wasn't a similar one or an extra that he had purchased. It was *his* jacket. The one that I wanted. There's just something about receiving an item from someone valuable in your life that they used to have and use.

Look at all the people who collect sports paraphernalia. People will spend an arm and a leg just to get the boxing gloves that Mike Tyson wore during his big fight or Derek Jeter's fielding glove.

We want what our heroes had and used. Well, Jesus has given us His peace—the exact one that He used and had Himself. What a gift! That gift surely surpasses any suit jackets or baseball gloves that this world can offer.

REAL OR FAKE?

But it's imperative that we know if there is a genuine peace that Jesus gives us, the world will try to give you a false peace. Whenever we go to dinner, I always get a soda with my meal. When I get really thirsty, that soda is like a drop of heaven to my taste buds. I'll drink the entire thing! But sooner or later, I'll want it refilled. It didn't actually quench my thirst, but it made me want more! That is what the world is constantly doing to us. It's giving us something that satisfies us for a moment but leaves us wanting more later. It's not permanent. It's like I try and I try and I try and I try, but I can't get no...well, you get the point.

If there is a genuine peace that Jesus gives us, the world will try to give you a false peace.

A great example of this is when you develop a headache and go straight to the Advil. It works for a few hours, but sooner or later, the headache comes back. Advil doesn't actually take the pain away; what it does is distract your brain from noticing the pain. May I submit to you that if Advil can make your brain focus on something other than the pain, how much do you think Jesus can? Why do we rely on worldly fixes to give us relief?

Why do we have to watch that certain video when no one is looking to get relief? Why do we have to smoke that blunt to get some relief? Why do we have to drink that liquor to escape? All of these things are temporal things that the world encourages you to do to manage the stress and pain of life.

But what if there was something that was permanent and had no lingering effects? What if you could experience an escape without waking up with a hangover?

Jesus offers us a peace so perfect and pure that it's all we need to "escape" and feel true relief. Jesus said that His yoke is easy and light (Matthew 11:30). We can experience true life-altering peace when we are in Jesus Christ.

IT'S IN BETWEEN YOUR EARS

Ultimately, the peace Jesus gives to us is peace that enables us not to let our hearts be troubled. It doesn't mean that bad things won't happen, but we've been given the ability and the choice to remain in Jesus' peace that He gives to us.

> *These things I have spoken to you, that in Me you may have peace. In the world you will have tribulation; but be of good cheer, I have overcome the world.*
>
> **John 16:33**

It's only when we are in Jesus that we can remain in His peace. A distinction is made between being in the world and being in Jesus. In the world, we will have tribulation, but in Jesus, we will have peace. Your positioning is the determining factor of whether or not you are remaining in peace.

My 17-month-old son, Matthew, is still discovering his emotions and what and who he is comfortable with. In the early stages of his development, anytime a stranger (specifically a man) would approach him to say hi, he would immediately begin crying. The interesting thing was that if he were sitting alone in the grocery cart or standing on the ground, he would be unsure and scared. However, if he was in mommy or daddy's arms, strangers could approach him, and he would be fine. What changed was not the circumstance but his position in that circumstance. As long as he had his mommy or daddy, he was going to be okay.

Many of us live life outside of our positioning in Christ and experience loss, hardship, pressure at work, and neglect in relationships. We develop emotions of fear and worry. Jesus said that in the world, bad things would happen, but we could experience peace. Your circumstances should not dictate your emotional state, and your emotions should not determine your life.

When you position yourself correctly in Jesus, the same losses, hardships, pressures at work, and neglect in relationships are still going to be there. They don't diminish into thin air. But you are now in the arms of your Father, who loves you. You become safe and secure regardless of what is happening around you.

God promised us that even though the mountains will depart and the hills will be removed, His kindness will never leave us, and His promise of peace will never be removed (Isaiah 54:10). God already placed the promise of peace inside us when Jesus entered our hearts. We don't need to ask God for peace—we've already got it! Next time something troubling comes your way, I want you to do two things.

Circumstances should not be dictating what you are feeling emotionally.

First, I want you to position yourself correctly in Jesus. How do you do that? Get your face out of Facebook and get your face in His Book. Find scriptures that correspond with who you are in Christ. The good news for you is that we have a cheat sheet on our website called *Confession Cards* that you can place on your bathroom mirror, in your car, on your nightstand, or wherever it is that you will see it the most. Start reciting these verses, get them into your heart, and believe what they say about you.

Secondly, I want you to stop asking God for peace. I know that sounds counterintuitive, but remember, you don't need to ask God to give you something that He has already given you! Imagine if I were to hand you my wallet. Now you have full possession of my wallet. What do you think my reaction would be if you then asked for my wallet (with it already in your full possession)? I'd look at you like you're dumb. I'd say, "What kind of question is that?"

If God could get confused, I believe He would be with the number of wrong prayers people pray. I can imagine Him being up in Heaven, bombarded with all these prayers of people asking Him to give them what He already provided, and looking to Jesus and saying, "Didn't you tell them that I already provided everything they would ever need?" You don't need more peace from God. What you need is a better understanding of what you already have because of Jesus.

Our spiritual warfare is not our in the heavenly places or in the cosmos. I believe that spiritual warfare happens in between your ears! The mind is the battleground, and if you don't take control of the way you think, it will damage you. So many people are being oppressed by the devil, and they think that there is nothing anyone can do about it.

The reality is the devil can't do anything to you without your consent and cooperation. If you don't know who you are and what you have because of Jesus Christ, you'll continue to lose the battle every time. Most Christians are not as oppressed as they think they are.

Sometimes, we will fall into the temptation to think, "If my circumstances improve, then I will have less stress in my life." That is the lie from the pit of hell. Your circumstances should not dictate your blood pressure. God said that He would never remove His covenant of peace. So, if you aren't in peace, it's not because God removed it from you; you removed yourself from Him. We have to remain in Him to experience this supernatural peace. The world will try to offer a counterfeit peace, but Jesus offers lasting peace.

AN ARTESIAN WELL

In John, Jesus and the disciples traveled from city to city, and they ended up on the outskirts of a town called Samaria. Now, the Samaritans and the Jews did not like each other in the slightest. Jesus had been tired from traveling and rested at Jacob's well. While He was there, a Samaritan woman came out of the town to draw some water from the well. When she came near the well, Jesus asked her to give Him some water from that well.

Jesus was thirsty, but He was also looking for an opportunity to minister. She was hesitant at first, asking Him why He was even talking to her since she was a Samaritan and He was a Jew, but eventually, Jesus got to His main point.

> *Jesus answered and said to her, Whoever drinks of this water will thirst again, but whoever drinks of the water that I shall give him will never thirst. But the water that I shall give him will become in him a fountain of water springing up into everlasting life.*
>
> **John 4:13-14**

Jesus was telling this woman that there is a peace that the world will try to offer us. It's temporal. But He offers a peace that is everlasting. Do you see what happens when we step out of our position in Jesus? We lose the benefits of what only He can offer.

It's like pulling a fish out of water. It doesn't matter how hard that fish tries; it will never be able to breathe outside of its environment. Likewise, Christians all over the world are trying to operate and live their lives outside of their natural environment (which is in Christ) and expect good results. It's only when you go back into the environment that you were created for you'll experience life and peace.

Jesus said that the water that He gives to us will become a fountain inside of us. The illustration that He was using here was that of an artesian well. An artesian well doesn't need a water pump to draw the water out. In fact, it doesn't need anything to draw the water out.

The water automatically gushes out of the well under certain conditions. An artesian well works by having a water table sitting above the well itself. Refer to the diagram below.

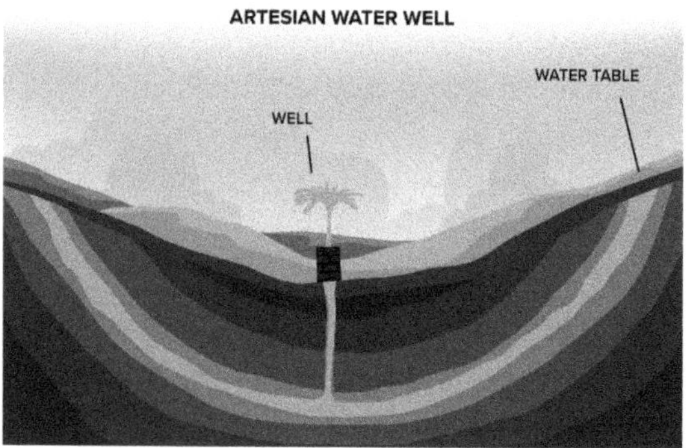

As long as the water table (or the source of the water) is above the well, gravity will push the water out of the well. But the moment that the well rises above the water table, it dries up.

Jesus said, "The water that I shall give Him..." He is our water table. He is our source. We are the well that waters other people.

As long as He is above us and we are positioned correctly in Him, we will never run dry.

DON'T LET HIM PASS YOU BY

The moment we try to do things with our own strength and ability, we stop experiencing this supernatural flow of life. Solving everything by our own means is like raising the well above the water table. The flow cannot continue. We cannot expect to be at peace in life when we are constantly using our own strength. In fact, there is a story about the disciples that resonates with this very "well." Get it?

In Mark's Gospel, Jesus and His disciples were wrapping up a huge miracle. They just fed over 15,000 people with five loaves of bread and a couple of fish. The Bible's translators denote this miracle as the feeding of the 5,000, but that was only the men, not including the women and the children. After this amazing event, He told His disciples to get into a boat and cross over the Sea of Galilea to Bethsaida.

While the disciples listened and set sail, Jesus went up to a mountain to pray. If Jesus needed alone time with God the Father, I think we do, too. But that's a topic for a different chapter. As the disciples were rowing and Jesus was praying, a huge storm came against the disciples on the water.

> *Now when evening came, the boat was in the middle of the sea; and He was alone on the land. Then He saw them straining at rowing, for the wind was against them. Now about the fourth watch of the night He came to them, walking on the sea, and would have passed them by.*
>
> **Mark 6:47-48**

I mentioned this earlier, but it says, "Now about the fourth watch of the night He came to them" (Mark 6:48). Earlier, it said that Jesus sent them out when the evening had approached. The fourth watch of the night was somewhere between 3 and 6 a.m. I can't imagine rowing for 10 straight hours and barely making it a few miles across the Sea of Galilee. The disciples were struggling big time and had little results.

They were relying on themselves to get out of that storm. It said that Jesus came walking to them on the water and "would have passed them by." I feel that many of us are doing the same thing. We are trying to get ourselves out of bad situations and make things happen in our own power, and we miss Jesus coming to help us every single time. Jesus will let us struggle every single time if we never acknowledge Him. He is a gentleman. He will never force Himself on us without our consent. If we don't take time to acknowledge Him and the need we have for Him, He will pass us by and wait for us on the other side (if we even get there).

Jesus will let us struggle every single time if we never acknowledge Him.

My friend Dustin Barker has a four-word prayer that can change your life. It goes, "Lord, I acknowledge you." That simple prayer can change your life. It might not change the circumstances that you're facing, but it will change your reactions to them. I like to put this concept into an equation to help people understand it better.

Our Works Before His Presence = Worry

His Presence Before Our Works = Peace

Every time we put our works before acknowledging Him for help, we will always wind up stressed and worried. But when we say, "Lord, I can't do this on my own. I need your help," He will always show us what to do. God has never let me down yet, and He never will.

CHAPTER 9 DISCUSSION:

1. What does Proverbs 23:7 mean to you in the context of controlling your thoughts and mindset? How does this verse relate to your daily life?
2. In what ways do you think society's view of being a product of our environment contrasts with the biblical perspective presented in this chapter?
3. How do you position yourself correctly in Jesus during difficult times? What specific practices or scriptures help you stay grounded in His peace.
4. Reflect on the statement, "Our Works Before His Presence = Worry, His Presence Before Our Works = Peace." Can you share an experience where you've seen this principle at work in your life?
5. How do you interpret Jesus' statement in John 16:33 about having peace in Him despite tribulation in the world? How can this promise influence your response to challenges?

REFLECT ON WHAT THE HOLY SPIRIT SPOKE TO YOU IN THIS CHAPTER:

Chapter 10

Soul Peace

While the world will offer you a false sense of peace, Jesus will offer you true peace. As believers, there should be a difference between how the world responds to things and how we respond to certain things. The world's primary response to tough situations is usually fear and panic. This usually leads to them finding a coping mechanism to get them through it. It's like how Linus van Pelt from Charlie Brown always carried around a security blanket. People find ways to cope with their problems in life.

Jesus never told us to cope with the issues of life. In fact, he never told us to find ways to manage our stress, either. In modern society, we are given so many different ways to manage stress. Notice how they don't offer you a way to get rid of it. They just want you to manage it. But what if I told you that there is a better way to live? Stress is not yours to manage. It's Jesus' to remove!

> *Therefore, having been justified by faith, we have peace with God through our Lord Jesus Christ, through whom also we have access by*

> *faith into this grace in which we stand, and rejoice in hope of the glory of God. And not only that, but we also glory in tribulations, knowing that tribulation produces perseverance; and perseverance, character; and character, hope.*
>
> **Romans 5:1-4**

How do we get to a place in our lives where we can "glory in tribulations"? The New Living Translations says, "*We can rejoice, too, when we run into problems and trials.*" It seems that in the moment of adversity, the last thing we want to do is rejoice. We want to sulk and cry and have everyone feel bad for us. Some of us go straight to Facebook and post about our sufferings so that we can get pity comments and feel better about ourselves. That is horrible.

REJOICING DURING HARDSHIP

Paul says that we can rejoice when things come against us. We aren't rejoicing because of the affliction, but we rejoice because we know that we always have the victory. This is something that not everyone can say about themselves. It's very easy to rejoice when everything is going well. But when things begin to head downhill, we fall apart.

This all has to do with your mindset. What you focus on in times of distress matters. If you choose to focus on all of the negatives that you are surrounded by, it will inevitably get you down. But if you choose to focus on the truth–the same truth that Paul focused on—you can't help but rejoice.

Paul continued in the next few verses. He was comparing how much God loved us when we were still sinners to how much more we are loved by God as His children. That's the overarching reason why Paul could rejoice during tribulation.

Think about this: if God was able to bring the worst of the sinners (Paul) into redemption and salvation, how much more could God work every bad situation around for his good now that he is a redeemed, reconciled man of God? And the same goes for us today. If God could take us at our worst and turn our lives around for the good, how much more can we trust God to get us out of any bad situation now that we are His children? When you think about it in that light, it's much easier to rejoice, regardless of what comes against you.

The way the world deals with hardship is by embracing it. They embrace the sufferings and like to say, "What doesn't kill you makes you stronger." I often hear people say things like, "Diamonds are just pieces of charcoal that handled stress very well," and then try to relate it to whatever it is that they are going through. I understand what they are trying to say, but it's a wrong mentality. We aren't supposed to glorify the suffering. Paul didn't say that I glorify the tribulation. He said that we "glory *in* tribulation". There's a huge difference.

We can't avoid tribulation, but we can be victorious.

So, if the world deals with hardship that way, we need to operate differently. Instead of glorifying and embracing the hardship, we need to glorify and embrace the grace of God during trials. We cling to the one who can get us out of every storm. People like to take these verses and say that God is the one who brings hardship and suffering into our lives because it produces perseverance, character, and hope. Again, that is not what the scripture is teaching. We've already established a few chapters ago why tribulation happens.

Tribulation is an already existing factor in life. We can't avoid tribulation, but we can be victorious. We can actually make it to the other side better off than before because of God. That is why we rejoice. We can't simply sit back and embrace the difficulties we are facing. That is as foolish as a soldier in war embracing the enemy in battle because they're excited about the spoil to take if they are victorious. No, we fight and win the war then we can take the spoil. We don't embrace the cancer; we fight it. We don't embrace poverty; we fight against it. We don't embrace the generational curses; we fight them.

YOUR MIND IS THE MATTER

The devil does not come except to steal, kill, and destroy. He never comes to be a blessing in our life. He isn't putting hardship on a platter for us to enjoy so we can be better off. But we can know that if we fight and win the battle, we will be better off. We will be stronger than before. That is the mentality that we should have. We don't need to embrace the problems but embrace the one who gives us the grace to have victory over the enemy.

If the tribulations and hardships that we faced were the things that perfected us as Christians, then the entire body of Christ would be unstoppable. Those who have faced the biggest battles and hardest problems would be the greatest and strongest Christians. It's not the battle that perfects us but rather the preparation before the battle that does. It's the training in advance that makes a military strong.

A boxer trains for months in advance before stepping into the boxing ring. The fight doesn't make them stronger. It was the preparation beforehand. The fight only shows them and everyone else how well they were prepared. It builds confidence. Likewise, when we prepare our hearts and minds in the Word of God before any tribulations come our way, that is what makes us better in the end.

It is very possible for us to rejoice in any hardship the devil throws our way. It all depends on what you focus on. Like Paul, we can rejoice when it seems like everything is falling apart because we know how much God can use us regardless of what we are facing. It all depends on what your mind is focused on. This goes beyond "mind over matter" concepts. We aren't ignoring the problems or pretending they aren't there. That's called denial. Mind over matter can work to a degree, but the subject our mind is focused on is what's truly pivotal in our lives.

> *You will keep him in perfect peace, whose mind is stayed on You, because he trusts in You.*
>
> **Isaiah 26:3**

This scripture clearly shows that our peace is not determined by our circumstances but by how much of our attention of fixed on Jesus or not. If we aren't experiencing peace in our lives, it's because we aren't focused on Jesus. We have our attention on other matters. The reason why you are drowning in anxiety and fear is that your emotions follow what you think about. If you are constantly thinking about "what-if" scenarios and your mind wanders to the worst-case scenario, your emotions will follow its lead.

I've prayed with many people, and whenever people ask me to pray for their minds that they would have peace and stop worrying, I tell them no. It's not that I don't want to see them freed from this mind prison. But, praying for peace alone doesn't do anything. You have to take responsibility and control what you think about. Feelings of fear and worry have to go away when your mind is fixated on Jesus. God has not given us a spirit of fear but of power, love, and a sound mind (2 Timothy 1:7). That sound mind that you have is what you need to tap into.

FOCUS ON THE BALL

My dog Daisy is one of, if not the greatest dog I've ever had. She doesn't cause any issues, and she is so darn cute. Daisy loves to play, and she especially loves to play with anything shaped like a ball. It could be an actual ball or a balled-up sock. As long as it looks like a ball, she wants it.

Daisy doesn't like fireworks very much, and almost every night, neighbors pop them off and spook her. I can try to calm her down by petting her or giving her treats, but whenever I offer her a ball, she immediately snaps out of her fear every time. She becomes so fixated on that ball that nothing else seemingly matters. If a rubber ball can do that to an animal imagine how much more Jesus can do that for us when we choose to focus on Him more than our fireworks in life.

Psalm 112 says that the righteous will never be shaken and will not fear bad news. The reason is that they trust in the Lord! So, what happens when we are fearful about bad news? We've taken our eyes off Jesus. It's possible to get to a place in your walk with God where nothing shakes you, nothing worries you.

We have a woman in our church named Mary who serves on the prayer team and leads our church in communion every weekend. She always shares how she will get hit with bad news, yet she stays strong and at peace because this is a reality for her. She has become steadfast in the

Lord because she trusts in Him. Mary has one of the most intimate relationships with God the Father, God the Son, and God the Holy Spirit. No doubt that is why she is able to withstand all that she's faced.

I mean, in every single conversation you have with her, she brings up Jesus or "Papa God." She is a big inspiration to me and many others in our church because of her vibrant relationship with God. Some of the things that she has been through would cause most Christians to flee with their tails tucked underneath them, but not her. Mary has a rock-solid foundation with the Lord.

Nothing shakes you, nothing worries you when you trust in the Lord.

Jesus mentions this type of foundation in the Gospel of Matthew. He illustrates two men, a wise man, and a foolish man, by saying, "*Anyone who listens to my teaching and follows it is wise, like a person who builds a house on solid rock. Though the rain comes in torrents and the floodwaters rise and the winds beat against that house, it won't collapse because it is built on bedrock*" (Matthew 7:24-25). This expresses that if anyone not only hears the truth found in God's Word but does what it says, they will be rock solid and nothing can shake them. Kind of like Mary.

But then Jesus said, "*Anyone who hears my teaching and doesn't obey it is foolish, like a person who builds a house on sand. When the rains and floods come and the winds beat against that house, it will collapse with a mighty crash*" (Matthew 7:26-27). Both men had to deal with the rains, floods, and winds. The difference wasn't the circumstances but in their foundation. It's much harder to put a foundation in rock than sand. Sand is easy to dig up and manipulate but it doesn't withstand storms. Rock, however, is much stronger but it takes more effort to manipulate and build on. Most Christians are taking the road that requires less effort on their part just to get by. But when the hardships come, they are destroyed like the foolish man's house.

Becoming free from worry and anxiety isn't done by prayer alone; it's done by keeping your mind fixated on Jesus. If you are dealing with mental health issues, I'm not a psychiatrist so don't take this as professional advice, but what you really need is Jesus. Whether or not you want to take medication is ultimately your decision. But you need to understand that God has given you a sound mind. It's already a part of you. It's a reality right now in your born-again spirit. You have a sound mind.

> *For God did not give us a spirit of timidity (of cowardice, of craven and cringing and fawning fear), but [He has given us a spirit] of power and of love and of calm and well-balanced mind and discipline and self-control.*
>
> **2 Timothy 1:7 AMPC**

In the Greek, this verse is saying that God has given you a calling to soundness of mind, moderation, and self-control. You need to understand that a peaceful mind belongs to you. You can't keep a bird from flying over your head, but you can keep it from nesting in your hair! Likewise, you can't stop negative thoughts from coming, but you can keep them from planting into your heart. You can't control certain situations from happening, but you can control what you think about it.

> *Those who live as their human nature tells them to, have their minds controlled by what human nature wants. Those who live as the Spirit tells them to, have their minds controlled by what the Spirit wants.*
>
> **Romans 8:5 GNT**

The list can go on with scriptures telling you that your life is going in the direction of what your mind is focused on. It's simple. If you are focused on the carnal–the flesh–your life is going to be controlled by the carnal. If you are focused on the Spirit–the things of God–your life will be controlled by the Spirit. That's not so bad, right? You might think, *so what that every once in a while I focus more on the carnal than on the spirit?* The next verse isn't so nice. In the Amplified Classic, it says,

> *Now the mind of the flesh [which is sense and reason without the Holy Spirit] is death [death that comprises all the miseries arising from sin, both here and hereafter]. But the mind of the [Holy] Spirit is life and [soul] peace [both now and forever].*
>
> **Romans 8:6 AMPC**

The mind of the Spirit is life and *soul* peace. What is the soul of a human, and why does it matter whether it's peaceful or not? Your soul is the most important part of your physical being. When God made you, He made you as a three-part being. You are a spirit, you have a soul, and you live in a body–spirit, soul, and body.

Your soul comprises your mind, your will, and your emotions. The mind is where your thoughts are formed, your will is where you make life-altering decisions (and small ones like which toppings to put on your pizza), and your emotions are where you feel. Your soul is more than just emotions as the moive *Inside Out* depicts. It's how you identify yourself. It's who you believe you are and most importantly, who you believe God is.

God wants us to be living at peace in our souls.

The Spirit of God living on the inside of you is able to give your entire soul peace. Peace in the way you think, peace in the way you feel, and peace in the way that you make decisions. The vast majority of Christians aren't in soul peace like they should be. They are more stressed than they should be, they are drowning in guilt and condemnation, and they are constantly making the wrong choices in life. That is not the way God intended our life to be. God wants us to be living at peace in our souls. So, how do we start experiencing this?

The Bible describes us as having many different parts that make us who we are. Before you accept Jesus into your heart and become a part of the family of God, you have a natural, carnal mind which leads to death. The moment you get saved or born-again, God literally gives you a brand new mind. This mind is called the mind of Christ (1 Corinthians 2:16). Before you get scared you off into thinking you're schizophrenic, this just means you have your own mind and Jesus' mind inside of you. The reason why many Christians aren't experiencing the life and peace that the Spirit offers is because they are still using their own carnal mind. They haven't become single-minded with Jesus.

CHOCOLATE LAVA CAKE

Have you ever had a best friend that whom you would finish each other's sentences? Or maybe someone that you're close with said something profound, and you were thinking the same thing? Every so often, my wife and I like to go on date nights with just the two of us. We have a second child on the way, so we want to make sure we are getting enough quality time with each other before our hands are even fuller. We like to spoil each other and go somewhere nice for dinner. After a romantic evening and delicious food, we still have some time to spare. We'll both look at each other and say, "Are you thinking what I'm thinking?" We both know at that moment exactly what we want next.

A chocolate lava cake from Chili's. I mean, come on, this isn't a romance novel that you're reading!

Stephanie and I are so close in our souls. We practically know what the other is thinking. That's what it's like being single-minded with Jesus. When you begin to become one with the mind of Christ, you'll begin to think like Him. When you think like Him, your emotions will begin to feel like Him, and then you can make decisions that Jesus would make. It's soul peace.

CHAPTER 10 DISCUSSION:

1. How does the world's response to tough situations, such as fear and panic, differ from the response Jesus expects from His followers?
2. The text emphasizes that Jesus does not want us to manage stress but to let Him remove it. How does this perspective change the way you handle stress and challenges in your life?
3. According to Romans 5:1-4, why is it important for Christians to "glory in tribulations"?
4. How does focusing on Jesus and His truths help shift your mindset during hardships?
5. How can preparing your heart and mind in God's Word beforehand help you face life's challenges more effectively?
6. The concept of having the mind of Christ is central to this chapter. How can you become more single-minded with Jesus, and what changes might you need to make in your daily life to achieve this?

REFLECT ON WHAT THE HOLY SPIRIT SPOKE TO YOU IN THIS CHAPTER:

Chapter 11

Anxious For Nothing

One of the things Jesus did a lot was pray. He prayed about everything. Prayer isn't limited to solitude and alone time with God in your prayer closet. It can consist of that, but prayer is also simply talking to God. In fact, Paul gives us a foolproof remedy for stress and anxiety in our lives, and it begins with prayer.

> *Be anxious for nothing, but in everything by prayer and supplication, with thanksgiving, let your requests be made known to God; and the peace of God, which surpasses all understanding, will guard your hearts and minds through Christ Jesus.*
>
> **Philippians 4:6-7**

First, Paul tells us to be anxious for nothing or to stop being anxious. How do we do that? It seems that everything is cause for stress and anxiety lately. There's a book called *Worried About Everything Because I Pray About Nothing* by Pastor Chad Veach. It's a great book. He talks about how prayer is life-changing and how to start implementing a good prayer life. Another book I would recommend you read is called *A Better Way To Pray* by Andrew Wommack. Prayer is an amazing tool that we have at our disposal to get rid of worry and stress. But a lot of people use prayer the wrong way.

Most people have a bad relationship with God and only use Him and abuse Him through prayer. To them, God is Jehova Gieco, and they only come to Him in prayer when they've run into an incident in life. I don't even remember the last time I talked to my insurance agent. I certainly don't call them just to chat or see how life's been. That is a subpar relationship with God that many people have. God wants all of you. He wants you to tell Him everything. He's so good that He wants to hear how your day has been even though He knows already. God doesn't get tired of you or bored of your stories. You're His everything.

Paul says that we should pray about *everything*, and then he tells us how to pray.

1. PRAYER AND SUPPLICATION

Let's first start by addressing what prayer is *not*. Prayer is not going to misinformed God and telling Him all about your issues. Again, that is the insurance company's job. God already knows your needs before you even have the need. Most of the time, when everything seems to be overwhelming, the first thing we tend to do is start our prayers with, "Dear Lord, I don't know what to do with all of this happening in my life. My car broke down, my house payment is late, the spouse took the kids, and I have a bald spot forming!" We whine and complain.

Recently, I saw a video that showed a very accurate picture of most Christian's prayer life. It was Jesus sitting at a dinner table, waiting for the person to show up. He waited and waited, and the server would come to the table to refill His water. After a few hours, the server asked Jesus, "Would you like the check?" but Jesus kept waiting for His guest to arrive. Finally, before the restaurant closed for the night, His guest finally arrived. He sat at the table, and before Jesus could greet them, they began to word-vomit and complain about every issue they faced that day. By the time they had finished, they had got up, said bye, and left.

That is not prayer. Your prayer life should reflect your relationship with Jesus. The word "prayer" is the Greek word *proseuchē*, which means to worship or praise. You can't complain about your issues while you worship God. Additionally, you can't worry about things and worship God at the same time. The same place in your soul where you worry is the same place where you worship God. So, the remedy to stop being anxious all of the time is to start worshiping God more.

Our prayers need to start with praising God first. That is the order that Paul gave us. He said, "By prayer *and* supplication." Supplication is the part of our prayer where the needs or issues are addressed. There's a strategy behind this order. When we praise God, the Bible says that we strengthen ourselves against the devil (Psalm 8:2, Matthew 21:16). The devil wants all of the praise that he can get. And if he can't get you to praise him directly, he'll get you to praise him indirectly through your issues. When we magnify our issues and problems and complain to God about them, we are worshiping them. But when we start our prayer by worshiping God regardless of our issues, when we glory in our tribulation, it strengthens us.

The remedy to stop being anxious all of the time is to start worshiping God more.

If you start your prayers right with praise and worship to God, by the time you get to the supplication, it will look very insignificant compared to God. When you reflect on how good God's been to you and all of the blessings He has given you, you'll build up your faith.

A great example of this in the Bible is when Paul and Silas were thrown in prison for nothing! Paul and Silas were traveling, preaching the Gospel when Paul received a vision of a man in a place called Macedonia. The man was asking Paul to come and travel to their city. Paul and Silas discerned that this was the Holy Spirit directing them to their next destination, and they went.

As they traveled through Philippi, they were met by a woman who was a fortune-teller. She was possessed by the devil–so are those who practice the same things she practiced, such as horoscopes, reading of tea leaves, tarot cards, reading of palms, crystal balls, and on and on. She used these demonic powers to bring the men who were her owner's money.

For many days, she followed Paul and Silas, saying things like, "These men are the servants of the Most High God, who proclaim to us the way of salvation" (Acts 16:17). She professed the truth, but she did it out of mockery and a wrong spirit. This goes to show that not everyone who says the right thing is from God.

After a few days, Paul becomes annoyed with this woman and casts out the demon who is influencing her. When her masters saw that she was no longer under that demonic influence and wasn't usable for their gain anymore, they got really upset. They weren't mad at the woman but mad that they couldn't make any more money. Because of all of this, they took Paul and Silas, threw them in front of the leaders and rulers of their city, and started making false accusations against them.

God's power can be released through prayer and worship.

If you think that's bad, it gets worse. Paul and Silad are then beaten, whipped, and cast into prison. They weren't just in a holding cell; they were taken to the "inner prison" (Acts 16:24), where there was no sunlight or visibility. Then, they were put in stocks, which were Roman instruments of torture that had holes in them for their arms, heads, and feet. In the darkest place in the prison, at the darkest time in the night, Paul and Silas were wrongfully thrown in prison and left there to die. They had all the reasons to complain and be upset about their circumstances, but they chose to do something different.

They decided to praise God and worship Him in the middle of all of their hardship. I doubt that they had any "feelings" of wanting to praise God, but they did it anyway. They weren't praising God for the circumstances but in spite of them. Because of it, a supernatural earthquake shook the entire prison, loosened its chains, freed it from the stocks, and opened the prison doors. This wasn't just a coincidence. This was a supernatural earthquake. God's power can be released through prayer and worship. One of the most fascinating parts of this story is that after Paul and Silas were freed from their bonds, they didn't leave. This shows us that they weren't just praising God to get them out of a bad situation but because they truly desired to worship Him.

2. WITH THANKSGIVING

An attitude of gratitude can go a long way. Studies from Harvard University show that having gratitude in your life can increase its quality. In fact, two psychologists, one from the University of California and the other from the University of Miami, have researched and tested this idea.

> In one study, they asked all participants to write a few sentences each week, focusing on particular topics.
>
> One group wrote about things they were grateful for that had occurred during the week. A second group wrote about daily irritations or things that had displeased them, and the third wrote about events that had affected them (with no emphasis on them being positive or negative). After 10 weeks, those who wrote about gratitude were more optimistic and felt better about their lives. Surprisingly, they also exercised more and had fewer visits to physicians than those who focused on sources of aggravation.[1]

If you are alive today, there are many things for which you can be thankful. Having difficulties being thankful is not a result of having fewer things to be thankful for but because it's a practice that you have to develop. If you are not naturally grateful for things, it's going to take some work to develop that type of attitude. In our prayer lives, thankfulness must be present. When you start praising God, thanksgiving should naturally begin to arise.

The result of praying the right way should end in peace. If you aren't at peace after you pray, chances are that you didn't pray the right way! Just because you start your prayer with, "Dear Lord," and end it

1 Harvard Health Publishing. (2021, August 14). Giving thanks can make you happier. Harvard Health. https://www.health.harvard.edu/healthbeat/giving-thanks-can-make-you-happier

with, "In Jesus' name, amen," doesn't mean you actually prayed. Praying should always result in you being at peace.

GET YOUR MIND OUT OF THE GUTTER

When you pray the right way, the peace of God will guard your heart and mind. Some of us are at a loss for words when we pray. If you need help with how and what to pray about, Paul gives us a prayer guide in the next verses.

> *Finally, brethren, whatever things are true, whatever things are noble, whatever things are just, whatever things are pure, whatever things are lovely, whatever things are of good report, if there is any virtue and if there is anything praiseworthy—meditate on these things.*
>
> **Philippians 4:8**

You can't keep a thought from entering your mind, but you can choose what you think. Most of us are not thinking about these things on a regular basis. If Christians were to meditate on these things like how we are supposed to, it would eliminate the majority of things that we allow in our heads that we call entertainment. We wouldn't be watching shows like *Game of Thrones*, which is filled with pornography and debauchery. We wouldn't be so engulfed with the latest political news. We wouldn't be listening to profanity in our music.

If you were to cut all of that out of your life and focus on things that are *pure, noble, just, pure, lovely, of good report, virtuous,* and *praiseworthy,* it would be impossible to stay worried. I once heard someone say, "If you aren't worried about life, it's because you aren't paying attention." What you are thinking about truly matters.

This is why I say that stress, worry, and anxiety can't be "prayed" away. You need to choose what you think about and what you pray about. Your circumstances can absolutely influence what you think about, but they don't directly impact your emotions. You're in control of those—at least, you should be. My prayer for you is that you will experience soul peace or be spiritually minded—peace in your mind, peace in your emotions, and peace in your decision-making.

> *And let the peace of God rule in your hearts, to which also you were called in one body; and be thankful.*
>
> **Colossians 3:15**

The word "rule" is the Greek word *brabeúō*, which literally means "to be an umpire" (Strong's Concordance). Now, I'm not too sure if Paul ever played baseball. However, it's more probable that we got the word "umpire" from this concept of ruling. In baseball, an umpire makes the final decisions concerning the game. When a pitch is thrown, the umpire will either call it a ball or a strike. Many times in the sport, players often disagree and argue with the umpire's decision; however, regardless of how much they disagree with the umpire's decision, the call stands. It's final.

Paul was saying that peace needs to be the umpire of our lives. It's not necessarily saying that we need to be peacemakers all of the time, but what it is saying is that peace needs to be the ruler of our decisions. This is a big issue if your emotions control you. Peace is not the absence of hardships; it's being in the presence of Jesus. It's thinking of things that are lovely and pure. It's being thankful and praising God first when you pray. It's keeping your mind focused on Jesus because you trust in Him. Peace should be the deciding factor in every single decision that you make in life. Not only when you have peace about a decision but also when you lack peace about a decision.

Peace is not the absence of hardships; it's being in the presence of Jesus.

As pastors, we have many opportunities to add a new element to service, start a new program, or do something someone else is doing. These might all be great and have good success elsewhere, but if we don't feel peace about them, we won't do them. I've been invited to speaking engagements that would pay handsomely, but because peace was not there, I didn't accept them.

Our lives are going to present us with so many different decisions to make. Where to move, who to marry, what church to attend, and if peace is not a factor in your decision-making, chances are you're going to make the wrong choice. This peace is available to all of us. And through keeping your mind fixated on Jesus and choosing what to think about, you too can experience this supernatural peace "which surpasses all understanding" (Philippians 4:7).

CHAPTER 11 DISCUSSION:

1. How does the analogy of Jesus waiting at a dinner table reflect common misconceptions about prayer?
2. According to the text, why is it important to start prayers with praise and worship before addressing personal needs or issues?
3. How does the story of Paul and Silas in prison illustrate the power of worship and prayer in difficult circumstances?
4. What does it mean for peace to be the "umpire" of our lives, and how can this concept influence our decision-making process?
5. How can focusing on gratitude and thanksgiving in our prayers impact our overall well-being and stress levels?
6. In what ways can changing what we think about and meditate on, as suggested by Philippians 4:8, transform our mental and emotional state?

REFLECT ON WHAT THE HOLY SPIRIT SPOKE TO YOU IN THIS CHAPTER:

Chapter 12

Called To Suffer

As a pastor, I've been privileged to be in front of hundreds of different people and give them the Gospel. It's been a blessing. One thing that I have discovered is that there are certain ways to gain easy applause from the congregation! In general, getting an applause can be easy. Imagine you're at a football game party, and everyone is there to support the best team in the league, the Raiders.

It's *easy* to get applause from everyone when you say, "Let me hear you shout if you love football!" There is no real effort that has to take place to get everyone to start shouting. The same can be true in the church as well. If you have a group of born-again believers together and say, "Come on, clap your hands if you love Jesus!" you will most likely get everyone to start applauding for Jesus. You can make anyone applaud if you know how to get them going. However, there is one topic in the church that doesn't get applauded, and that is suffering.

Not many people want to shout and holler about the topic of suffering because there are truths in it that might hurt a little bit, but if you grasp ahold of them and do not let them offend you, it can transform the way you deal with suffering, enlightening you and empowering you in ways you never thought possible.

The whole purpose of this book is to take control of your thought life and become more mindful of the way that you think. The way that your dominant thought is heading is the direction that your life will follow (Proverbs 23:7). So let's change the way that we think about suffering and what the Bible actually says about this subject. This change in perspective will not only motivate you but also inspire you to face suffering with a new understanding.

The Christian life is not pie in the sky by and by; it's steak on your plate while you wait.

The church as a whole fails to discuss this topic from the pulpit, and when it does preach on it, it usually does so from a false understanding. In this chapter, we will be addressing suffering and we are going to be talking about it in a way that you might not have heard before. It's going to challenge some of our ways of thinking and hopefully change them. It might even seem completely off from what you believe is true or what you've been taught, but I can guarantee you that it's right on.

How would it sound if you could become perfected, established, strengthened, and settled in life? Not many believe that these things are achievable in this life. In fact, too many Christians believe that someday, when we all get to heaven, only then will we be able to experience heaven. The Christian life is not pie in the sky by and by; it's steak on your plate while you wait. You can experience a heaven-on-earth reality in this life. That's the way God intended us to live.

However, this perfecting, establishing, strengthening, and settling does come with a price–suffering. But it's not in the way that you think. I once served under some leaders in the church who believed that you have to pay your dues to climb the leadership ladder in the church. They believed that the only way God could use you was if you went through the fire and the flames of life. Many times, those fires and flames they believed we must go through were caused by God to test us.

The New Testament does say that suffering and trials do test us. They test to see whether or not our faith is genuine or fake, but the New Testament *never* says that those tests are from God.

> *Be sober, be vigilant; because your adversary the devil walks about like a roaring lion, seeking whom he may devour. Resist him, steadfast in the faith, knowing that the same sufferings are experienced by your brotherhood in the world.*
>
> **1 Peter 5:8-9**

The devil is described as "like a roaring lion" looking to devour someone. This is huge. This means that the devil is *not* a roaring lion but is an imposter. He is pretending to be something that he is not. If the devil were a lion, he would be a toothless lion. He can't do anything to us without our consent and cooperation. However, he is still a threat to us, and that is why Peter says that we need to be sober and vigilant or have clear judgment and be ready to fight.

One of the main things that the enemy likes to do in our lives is to try to get us in isolation in our minds. Before a lion kills their prey, they isolate the weakest link. The enemy will find someone who is weak in their faith, someone who is not being mindful of his deception, and he will isolate them. The way that he isolates us is by sending thoughts that say, "No one has ever gone through what you're going through," or "You're alone in this struggle." And he tries to isolate us and tell us lies.

If he can get you to believe that you're the only one going through what you're going through, then he can isolate you. The way that you can stop that belief from forming is through understanding that "the same sufferings are experienced by your brotherhood in the world." In other words, you're not alone! What you're facing right now, there have been others who have faced it.

Even if you don't know anyone who has gone through the same thing you've gone through, Hebrews 4:15 says that Jesus was tempted in all things like us so that He could empathize with us. He gets us! They might not be exactly identical to your situation, but realize that the devil has no new tricks in his arsenal. He uses the same gifts that are wrapped in a different package. We've talked about why the devil does this, and it's to get the Word of God that you've planted out of your heart so that you aren't an effective Christian. Don't let him deceive you.

> *But may the God of all grace, who called us to His eternal glory by Christ Jesus, after you have suffered a while,* **perfect, establish, strengthen, and settle you.** *To Him be the glory and the dominion forever and ever. Amen.*
>
> **1 Peter 5:10-11**

"After you have suffered a while." What does this mean? There have been so many misinterpretations of this verse over the past centuries. About a year ago or more, I had a lady come to me after a church service and give me a "Word from God." At this point in my life, things were looking great. The church was growing, and my family was healthy, finances were great, and life was good. She took me outside and began to tell me what she believed was a Word from God.

She had told me some concerning things about my life. Things that would make a normal person fall into fear, but I'm not normal. After that, she hugged me, said nice things about me, and then left. I immediately dismissed what she had told me because I knew that it was not from God. Without going into too much detail, she basically told me that I was going to have to suffer big time in order for God to use me and grow our church. Before you receive a word that someone speaks over you, you need to make sure that your spirit bears witness to their spirit. If it doesn't, then dismiss that word. What you don't know is that this woman is a very nice, generous, and *emotional* woman. And most of the time, when people allow their emotions to drive their train, they are misled into doing the wrong things.

The fact is, suffering is a real, present reality that will come into our lives if it hasn't already, but we need to identify the right kind of suffering and not allow the devil to mislead us into the wrong type. So, what does suffering look like according to the Bible? Believe it or not, if you read the Bible in-depth, you'll find the answers!

DO WE ALL HAVE TO SUFFER?

Let's first start by addressing the elephant in the room. If you are a believer, yes, you need to suffer. If you don't suffer the right way, you'll suffer the wrong way. The Bible actually tells us that there is suffering that is according to the will of God, which means it is God's will for us to suffer.

> *Therefore let those who suffer according to the will of God commit their souls to Him in doing good, as to a faithful Creator.*
>
> **1 Peter 4:19**

The Bible is very clear that there is a type of suffering according to God's will. However, many Christians have taken different bits and pieces from the Bible that have anything to do with suffering and pieced them all together to say that the suffering that we face is hardship, sickness, poverty, and everything in between. But that is not what the scripture teaches when it comes to what and how we suffer as Christians.

> *Blessed be the God and Father of our Lord Jesus Christ, who according to His abundant mercy has begotten us again to a living hope through the resurrection of Jesus Christ from the dead, to an inheritance incorruptible and undefiled and that does not fade away, reserved in heaven for you, who are kept by the power of God through faith for salvation ready to be revealed in the last time. In this you greatly rejoice,* **though now for a little while, if need be, you have been grieved by various trials**, *that the genuineness of your faith, being much more precious than gold that perishes, though it is tested by fire, may be found to praise, honor, and glory at the revelation of Jesus Christ.*
>
> **1 Peter 1:3-7**

This sounds a lot like what we read earlier. Why will we suffer? The suffering that we go through is considered the trial of our faith, and the purpose of it is to test whether or not our faith is genuine. If there is genuine faith, then there is fake faith. It's pretty easy to fake faith and quote a few scriptures. But once the hardship comes, what happens when you have fake faith?

THE TRIAL OF YOUR FAITH

Back in 2019, before COVID hit the USA, there were a lot of "faith" preachers who came out with bold statements about how they believed in healing and that they were not going to be affected by this worldwide virus. Shortly after, the World Health Organization (WHO) issued an order that churches and places of business needed to close their doors and stop having large gatherings to "stop the spread." Well, those same faith preachers who were once boldly declaring what they believed ended up closing the doors to their church "acting in wisdom." Call it what you want, but that is simply fake faith. So don't mistake me for saying suffering exists without a purpose because there is a purpose in it.

The purpose is to see whether or not your faith is true or fake. But what the scripture doesn't say is "who" is sending the trials, which has caused many to believe that God is sending the trials to test your faith. In the Old Testament, there is a story of these three men: Shadrach, Meshach, and Abednego. These three men loved God and served Him, but the king of Babylon, Nebuchadnezzar, wanted them to bow down and worship an idol that was over 100 feet tall and made out of solid gold. Some simple math shows that 3% of the total world supply of gold went into making this statue.

King Nebuchadnezzar had made a decree in all of the land that stated everyone needed to bow down and worship this idol at his command, and if they didn't obey, they would be thrown into a fiery furnace. And Shadrach, Meshach, and Abednego refused to worship that idol. They were faithful to God even though they would face real consequences. The king takes all three of them and threatens them before he throws them in the fire, and he stops to give them one last chance to bow down or be killed. But they still refused and only worshiped the one true God. King Nebu-

That is the purpose of trials and suffering: to test if your faith is genuine."

chadnezzar became even more furious and demanded that the furnace would be turned up seven times hotter than it already was. As one of the guards opened the furnace, he died because it was so hot. These three men get thrown into the fiery furnace, and the Bible says that as they were in there, those on the outside looked inside and saw four people standing in the furnace.

After they saw this, King Neb ordered his men to remove them from the furnace. When they came out, he noticed that the fire did not consume them, and they didn't even smell like smoke. This was a supernatural intervention from God. Because of this, King Neb realized that their God was the one true God. Let me ask you this. What was more valuable to them? The one-hundred-foot golden idol or their faith? Shadrach, Meshach, and Abednego were literally thrown into a fiery trial for their faith. God wasn't the one who threw them in the fire, but He was there with them, protecting them from the fire. Their faith was more valuable than a golden idol. That is the purpose of trials and suffering: to test if your faith is genuine.

Before we go down this road of no return, let's discuss what suffering does not include and what it should never include. Whatever Jesus redeemed us from on the cross, we are *not* to suffer from it.

1. He bore our sins and the punishment for our sins.

We don't have to suffer from guilt and condemnation when we mess up (because we will), but we can instead experience life and peace because of Jesus' sacrifice on the cross. God can and will still use you to make a big difference in this life, regardless of who you are. Our identity is in Jesus, not in our works. This is evident when we drink the juice during the Holy Communion.

2. He bore our sicknesses and diseases.

The other part of the Holy Communion is when we partake of the bread, which represents the body of Jesus that was beaten and bruised for you. If Jesus' blood was what washed our sins away, then the body has to deal with our physical bodies being healed. He was beaten before His crucifixion so that we would be healed in our physical bodies (1 Peter 2:24, Psalm 103:3). We don't have to suffer from sickness or disease.

3. He bore our poverty and lack.

He became poor so that we could become rich (2 Corinthians 8:9). Poverty and lack are not blessings in disguise or otherwise. Many scriptures, like Psalm 23 and Philippians 4:19, illustrate how God will provide our wants and needs. Prosperity is a taboo subject in the church, but many truths in the Word show differently. Living in poverty is not God's will and is not something we need to suffer from.

4. He bore mental anguish.

The Bible says that the night before Jesus' crucifixion, while Jesus was praying, He began to sweat drops of blood (Luke 22:44). This medical condition is a rare condition called Hemochromatosis. According to the *National Library of Medicine* website, this condition occurs when capillary blood vessels that feed the sweat glands rupture, causing them to exude blood. It occurs under conditions of extreme physical or emotional stress.[1]

Jesus was facing more than just a death sentence. He was about to take on more health and spiritual issues than anyone else has ever faced. He bore turmoil in the mind, anxiety, depression, and every evil thought Jesus bore and conquered for us on the cross. We don't have to suffer from mental anguish.

So then, what on earth do we actually suffer from if Jesus did the suffering for us? If you didn't know, the first scripture we looked at in this chapter was the second half of the full text. We need to go back and find out what we missed.

1 American Psychiatric Association. (2009). Positive and negative cognitive-behavioral patterns in obsessive-compulsive disorder. Journal of Psychiatry & Neuroscience, 34(1), 1-2. Available at: https://www.ncbi.nlm.nih.gov/pmc/articles/PMC2810702/

The elders who are among you I exhort, I who am a fellow elder and a witness of the sufferings of Christ, and also a partaker of the glory that will be revealed: Shepherd the flock of God which is among you, serving as overseers, not by compulsion but willingly, not for dishonest gain but eagerly; nor as being lords over those entrusted to you, but being examples to the flock; and when the Chief Shepherd appears, you will receive the crown of glory that does not fade away. Likewise you younger people, submit yourselves to your elders. Yes, all of you be submissive to one another, and be clothed with humility, for God resists the proud, but gives grace to the humble. Therefore humble yourselves under the mighty hand of God, that He may exalt you in due time.

1 Peter 5:1-6

THE SUFFERING OF SUBMISSION

This passage of scripture contains many great truths and key elements. If Jesus bore most of the suffering, then the suffering we are called to do is the suffering of submission. Why is submission something that we have to suffer from?

Not everyone properly understands how to do it. Submission does not come naturally to the flesh because suffering requires humility. Notice how Peter starts it by saying that young people need to submit to older people, and then everyone needs to submit to each other. Then he tells you how we submit. Submission is only done through humility.

If you're advanced in your years, I'm sure it's very hard to want to willingly submit to someone who is younger than you. That's what was going on in the church that Timothy was in charge of in the Bible. In fact, Paul has to encourage Timothy and tell him to not let them despise his youth but instead be an example to them (1 Timothy 4:12). Timothy was a younger pastor at the time, and most of the church was older than him.

My wife and I have been in a similar situation since the start of our church in 2021. Most of our church members are more than double our age! Yet, we've been so blessed to have people willingly submit under our leadership. However, that is not always the case. I've had to face difficult situations where I was threatening to someone much older than me because I knew something about the Word that they didn't know. But, if we can learn to be submissive to one another, regardless of age, it will go a long way in our lives.

> *Yes, all of you be submissive to one another, and* **be clothed with humility**, *for God resists the proud, but gives grace to the humble.*
>
> **1 Peter 5:5b**

So why is submission something that we have to suffer from? Because you have to be willing to humble yourself. You have to put on humility. What does humility say? "Regardless of your age and your experience, I'll do what you tell me to do." But Pride says, "Who are you to tell me what to do?" I've noticed that it's a lot easier to "submit" when you get paid for it at work. It's a lot easier when you have a boss who is younger than you, telling you what to do, but then they give you a paycheck for it on the 1st and 15th of the month.

How about when it needs to be done in your church? Or what about when it's in your family or friend group? It's a lot harder because you know them personally. You know their tendencies and habits. Regardless, we are all required to be submissive to one another because God has granted all of us the same grace, faith, wisdom, understanding, and every other spiritual blessing. No one is better than the other in His kingdom.

> *But He gives more grace. Therefore He says: God resists the proud, but gives grace to the humble. Therefore submit to God. Resist the devil and he will flee from you.*
>
> **James 4:6-7**

THE SUFFERING OF RESISTING

There is the suffering of submission, and then there is the suffering of resisting. Why are these both considered suffering? Because your flesh does not want to do either of these things. Your flesh doesn't want to submit to other people, and your flesh doesn't want to resist the devil! When the devil tries to put a sickness on your body, the last thing that your flesh wants to do is resist it. Most of the time, we want to run straight to the couch, call in for work, and binge-watch our favorite show all day long. There is hard work that needs to be done when it comes to resisting.

Before we discuss more details about resisting, we must understand something crucial to our spiritual lives. You cannot resist the devil if you have not submitted yourself to God.

> Submit to God: to arrange under, to subordinate, to put in subjection, to subject one's self, obey, to submit to one's control, to yield to one's admonition or advice, to obey, be subject.

This word was a Greek military term meaning "to arrange [troop divisions] in a military fashion under the command of a leader." Whenever you see the word "submit" in the Bible, this is exactly what it means. To arrange under someone else's leadership.

> *Therefore, since Christ suffered for us in the flesh, arm yourselves also with the same mind, for he who has suffered in the flesh has ceased from sin, that he no longer should live the rest of his time in the flesh for the lusts of men, but for the will of God.*
>
> 1 Peter 4:1-2

When you made Jesus Lord of your life, you submitted yourself to Him and to live a godly life. Living for your own self is over the moment you become saved, and living for Him is all that we will ever do. This doesn't mean that we will never have any more fun in life. In fact, the opposite is true. The real fun can begin! The amount of journeys that I have been on with the Lord is far greater than the dumb things I did before I was saved. But when we truly submit to living for God, what we are doing is bringing our own will *under* the will

You cannot resist the devil if you have not submitted yourself to God.

of God. This is why we suffer "according to the will of God" (1 Peter 4:19).

As we continue this topic, we need to remember what the word "submit" means: to arrange under. We are called to submit and put our fleshy desires and what we want under what God wants for our lives.

CHAPTER 12 DISCUSSION:

1. How can understanding the biblical perspective on suffering transform the way we deal with hardships in our lives?
2. In what ways can the concept of submission to God and others challenge our natural tendencies and fleshly desires?
3. What are some practical steps we can take to resist the devil and his attempts to isolate us in our minds?
4. How can we discern between the right kind of suffering that aligns with God's will and the wrong kind of suffering that does not?
5. How does the story of Shadrach, Meshach, and Abednego illustrate the purpose of trials and suffering in testing the genuineness of our faith?
6. How can we apply the principles of humility and submission in our relationships within the church and our daily lives?

REFLECT ON WHAT THE HOLY SPIRIT SPOKE TO YOU IN THIS CHAPTER:

Chapter 13

The Suffering of Submission

It is often insinuated that submission and obedience go hand in hand, but that is not always the case. You can attempt to obey someone's leadership and guidance, but if you aren't doing it with a willing heart, resentment will follow suit. You might do what they tell you to do, but if you don't do it out of a submissive attitude, you will never benefit from it. The Apostle Paul actually deals with this idea concerning our giving and generosity. He says,

> *You must each decide in your heart how much to give. And don't give reluctantly or in response to pressure. For God loves a person who gives cheerfully.*
>
> **2 Corinthians 9:7 NLT**

Yes, the Bible instructs us to give our finances to advance His kingdom, but it does not say to give out of compulsion or force. Just because you give an offering and obey what the Word says, it doesn't necessarily mean that you gave properly. God cares more about the intentions of your heart than He does your actions. Likewise, in our obedience in every other area of life, He wants us to be willfully submissive.

In this chapter, I aim to delve into the concept of submission in three key areas. Understanding and practicing submission in all these areas can lead to a life filled with success and favor, as it aligns with God's plan for us. These areas are submitting to God's Word, submitting to God's Spirit, and submitting to God's people.

This is why it is important to submit to these areas. In order to fully understand God's plan for your life and what you're called to do, you have to be fully submitted to His Word. His Word is the instruction manual for our lives, and if we want to be victorious people, we need to follow the instructions. Then, submitting to His Spirit is a big one. It's easy to get into God's Word and read a few chapters a day, but doing what He says to do is a bit of a challenge for people.

God's Spirit is always leading and guiding us into all truth, so we need to be submissive to its leading. Lastly, we need to be submissive to His people. This is where I find it most difficult for many Christians to do. But it's imperative that we do so because God predominately moves and works in our lives through people. If you don't have a healthy relationship with submitting to people, you'll have difficulties experiencing God's best in your life.

SUBMITTING TO GOD'S WORD

> *Now when Jesus had entered Capernaum, a centurion came to Him, pleading with Him, saying, Lord, my servant is lying at home paralyzed, dreadfully tormented. And Jesus said to him, I will come and heal him. The centurion answered and said, Lord, I am not worthy that You should come under my roof. But only speak a word, and my servant will be healed. For I also am a man under authority, having soldiers under me. And I say to this one, Go, and he goes; and to another, Come, and he comes; and to my servant, Do this, and he does it.*
>
> **Matthew 8:5-9**

I mentioned this story earlier in this book, but we need to circle back to it because there are some details that were not discussed before. Remember that a centurion was a commander in the Roman army who had 100 soldiers under his leadership. He finds himself in a difficult situation and comes to Jesus saying, "Hey, my servant is sick! Do something about it!" and Jesus agrees to heal his servant. But the centurion's faith was at a greater place than most people Jesus had encountered at that time. All that he needed was a word from Jesus to believe that his servant would be healed. But look at the specific wording that he tells Jesus. He said, *"Lord, I am not worthy that You should come under my roof"* (Matthew 8:8).

When the Lord revealed this to my heart, it changed the way I understood submission. Here's a respected centurion who is in charge of at least 100 soldiers, and they listen to any command that he makes. If anything, this man should have felt *worthy* to tell Jesus what to do. But instead, here he is at Jesus' feet, saying, "I'm not worthy." The recognition of knowing that he was not worthy of having Jesus come *under* him, *under* his desires, *under* his will, was what I believe determined the outcome of this story/ This man was ready to submit to Jesus's word.

We don't get to resist the devil until we've fully submitted to God's Word.

What he believed and anticipated would happen was solely accomplished through the submission of the Word. In the Gospel of John, Jesus is referred to as the Word of God. He was in the beginning of all things, and all things were made through Him (John 1:3). In the book of Genesis, we see that God created everything that we know and love today through words. Jesus was the Word of God that became flesh (John 1:14). So Jesus is literally the Word of God.

We see why the centurion believed in submitting to Jesus, the Word of God. The centurion said, *"For I* ***also*** *am a man under authority, having soldiers under me"* (Matthew 8:9). The centurion said that he *also* was *under authority*. Why did he say it in this manner? He recognized that Jesus was a man under the authority of someone else. Jesus had authority *over* sickness because He was a man *under* God's authority.

Jesus was fully submitted to God's will. You can't be above unless you go beneath.

In order for Jesus to do what Jesus could do, the centurion needed to be submitted under someone greater than himself. He needed to submit under a higher authority. Remember what we said about the Biblical definition of the word submit? It means to *arrange yourself under*. You can't be above whatever it is that you believe to be freed from unless you first go beneath God's authority. We don't get to resist the devil until we've fully submitted to God's Word. We have to get to a place where the Word of God is the final authority in our lives. Whatever it says to do, we do. Whoever it says that we are, we are. God's Word must be true before everything else in our life (Romans 3:4).

The reason why this centurion was in charge of over 100 soldiers was because he was under someone else's authority who was greater than him. Our authority over Satan comes from God's authority over us. If you don't submit to God's authority and try to exercise authority over the devil, it's like charging the gates of hell with a water pistol. You'll lose every time. Unfortunately, that is where a lot of Christians are. They try to resist, and they try to stand fast against the attacks of the devil, but they aren't rooted and grounded in God's Word.

As the pastors of Deep Rooted Church, we have the authority to elect and ordain ministers of the Gospel. We can hire and fire staff as we please. When we hire someone on our staff, we have the authority to delegate certain responsibilities to them if we see fit. Once we give them authority to do certain things, they have the freedom to exercise that authority.

Without them being submitted to our leadership (which would be a requirement to be on staff), they have absolutely zero authority to exercise over anyone in the church. The only reason why they have this permission is because someone higher than them gave it to them. We need to be submitted to what God's Word says to operate in any sort of authority in this life. Without this submission, we are powerless.

SUBMITTING TO GOD'S SPIRIT

> *Father, if you are willing, please take this cup of suffering away from me. Yet I want your will to be done, not mine. Then an angel from heaven appeared and strengthened him.*
>
> **Luke 22:42-43 NLT**

This was one of the darkest moments of our Lord and Savior as He was on the earth. Before this prayer, Jesus asked Peter, James, and John (His disciples) to keep watch while He was praying. Everything that He was about to face, from His betrayal to His crucifixion, was in the forefront of His mind. His soul was "exceedingly sorrowful" (Mark 14:34), and He needed His friend's support.

The vast majority of people don't realize that Jesus had to deal with the flesh, just like the rest of us. He faced temptations in the wilderness for 40 days before He began His ministry and was tempted in all points so that we could go to Him for strength. Jesus was fully human and fully God on the inside. Jesus didn't perform all of His miracles by being God but by being a man with the power and Spirit of God operating through Him. He lived His entire life on the earth as a man operating in His flesh.

His flesh did not want to go on the cross and die. This is why He had prayed to God three times to remove the cup that He would have to partake of if it was God's will. He comes to a battle in His heart to listen to His flesh or follow the Spirit, and there's a point in this battle where He goes back to His disciples to find them asleep instead of praying and tells them, "Watch and pray, lest you enter into temptation. The spirit indeed is willing, but the flesh is weak" (Mark 14:38). Jesus was referring to Himself.

His Spirit was willing to do what God had called Him to do, but his flesh was weak. His flesh didn't want to. There will come a point in all of our lives when our flesh will not want to do something that our spirit wants to do and also a point where our flesh does want to do something that the spirit doesn't want to do. It's our job to listen to the Spirit of God inside of us. The Holy Spirit living on the inside of us always wants to do what God wants us to do. Our flesh will try to stop us, but we need to give voice to the Spirit. The Spirit is willing to go on a fast, but our flesh says, "I don't want to fast. I like food too much." The Spirit is always willing to pray for someone, but our flesh says, "I don't want to pray for them. I don't want to embarrass myself." Regardless of what your flesh does or doesn't want to do, we need to give voice to the Spirit. What is the Spirit trying to lead us into? We need to be fully submitted to God's Spirit.

SUBMITTING TO GOD'S PEOPLE

In the Old Testament, there's a story about Naaman, a commander of the Syrian army. The Bible describes Naaman as a "great and honorable man" and a "mighty man of valor" (2 Kings 5:1), but he also was dealing with a disease called leprosy. We don't really see many forms of leprosy today like there were in the Bible. In Naaman's day, leprosy would rot your skin away and, in some cases, cause body parts to dissolve or fall off. If someone was a leper, it wasn't hard to tell.

Naaman was respected and loved by many people, but he had to deal with this disease. There are a lot of people who have this type of "but" in their lives, too. Life might look good in every other area, but you're dealing with something that you can't seem to fix. Maybe everything at work is looking great, and your health is where you desired it to be for a while, but your marriage is falling apart. Or maybe the family is doing well, and the kids are on the right path, but your boss is giving you more stress than you can deal with. Whatever the case, most people live with "buts" in their lives like Naaman.

One of Naaman's servants told his wife that she knew of a prophet in Samaria who could heal him of his leprosy. I'm sure that night, there was some pillow talk with him and Mrs. Leprosy, and she told him all about this prophet who could heal him. He got some good news! So Naaman told his higher-up, the king of Syria, that he needed to take some sick leave to see the prophet. The king agreed and sent a letter to the king of Israel. Some miscommunication happened, and the king of Israel thought that Naaman had come to see him for healing.

Most people live with 'buts' in their lives like Naaman.

Have you ever been confused before and then ripped your clothes? Well, that's what the king of Israel did. When the healing prophet, Elisha, found out about this mishap, he told the king of Israel to send Naaman to his house, and he would heal him.

Naaman then departs for Elisha's house, and when he gets there, he has brought his entire ensemble with him. I mean, I'm talking about a live-action Aladdin type of ensemble when Prince Ali enters Agrabah. This guy came in with horses and chariots and not mention his ten changes of clothes (2 Kings 5:5).

The difference between Naaman and the centurion was that Naaman was the commander of the entire Syrian army, not just over 100 soldiers. Naaman's pride and self-respect were unmatched. When he arrives at Elisha's door, he was in for a rude awakening.

> *Then Naaman went with his horses and chariot, and he stood at the door of Elisha's house. And Elisha sent a messenger to him, saying, Go and wash in the Jordan seven times, and your flesh shall be restored to you, and you shall be clean. But Naaman became furious, and went away and said, Indeed, I said to myself, He will surely come out to me, and stand and call on the name of the Lord his God, and wave his hand over the place, and heal the leprosy. Are not the Abanah and the Pharpar, the rivers of Damascus, better than all the waters of Israel? Could I not wash in them and be clean? So he turned and went away in a rage.*
>
> **2 Kings 5:9-12**

Naaman's pride got hurt. He was expecting to meet Elisha but instead got a messenger. We get a little glimpse of what Naaman was thinking leading up to this. In his mind, he said to himself that Elisha would make some grand gestures and make a big spectacle to heal his leprosy, but when that didn't happen, he became angry. In order for us to see God work in our lives, we need to submit to the people that He has placed in our lives. Submitting does not hold people to unrealistic expectations, but it gives people the benefit of the doubt. Naaman was moments away from missing out on his healing, but something that he did was teach us a lesson to apply in our lives.

> *And his servants came near and spoke to him, and said, My father, if the prophet had told you to do something great, would you not have done it? How much more then, when he says to you, Wash, and be clean? So he went down and dipped seven times in the Jordan, according to the saying of the man of God; and his flesh was restored like the flesh of a little child, and he was clean.*
>
> **2 Kings 5:13-14**

Sometimes, we need an outside perspective on certain things. You'll never go far in life if your philosophy is "my way or the highway." Notice that the person that Naaman listened to was a mere servant. If Naaman was the commander of the entire army, then a servant was surely insignificant to him. The issue Naaman had wasn't his leprosy but his unwillingness to bring himself under Elisha's instructions. It shouldn't matter who the person is who's telling us what to do; if the instructions are from God, then we should be quick to humble ourselves.

Being in ministry my entire life, I've seen many people, and with those people, I've seen many character traits. It's heartbreaking in the church when there are people who genuinely love the church and want to serve, but as soon as they are asked to do something that they feel is beneath them, they react negatively, similar to Naaman. We've had to deal with those people on a frequent basis. If scrubbing the toilets is beneath you, then singing on the worship stage is above you. You can see what a person is really made of when they are asked to do something they think is beneath them.

The kingdom of God is not about position or hierarchy. It's about serving and submitting to God's Word, His Spirit, and His people. And until we can understand that, we will be in for a rough ride. Now, notice when Elisha asked Naaman to dip in the Jordan River. He had told him to go dip himself in the river seven times, and his flesh would be restored–not just healed from its condition but restored or made whole again. There is an illustration that God's trying to show us in this. When you dip yourself in the water, what is it that you are actually doing? You are going under the water. You're submitting.

I can just imagine Naaman going underneath the water the first time and then coming back up thinking, *now what?* Submit again. And he did this seven times. That goes to show us that submission is not a one and done thing. We don't get to say, "I have submitted before, so I don't have to do it ever again." If that's your mentality about submission, you never truly submitted to begin with. You don't get to say, "I've paid my dues, now I'm in charge." That is not submitting. Just like how Naaman dipped in the water seven times, after we submitted the first time, what do we do next? Submit again. Then what? Submit again. Okay, now what? Submit...again. Because we don't get to resist the devil until we have fully submitted ourselves to the things of God.

If scrubbing the toilets is beneath you, then singing on the worship stage is above you.

This is what the suffering of submission looks like. After Naaman had finally submitted and listened to the man of God, it says that "his flesh was restored like the flesh of a little child." This refers to complete wholeness. Perhaps we can say that after he suffered a while, the God of all grace perfected, established, strengthened, and settled him. This didn't happen because of the suffering of his leprosy but of his submission. Humbling himself from his position of power to someone needing help.

If you don't think submission is hard, you haven't truly submitted. And something that we all have to remember is that no one can force you to submit. That is not submission, that is abuse. No one can make you submit. Not even God. Submitting can only come when you decide to do it. God will not make you submit to Him by putting you through a trial. You have to choose to submit to Him in order to receive all that He wants you to receive.

CHAPTER 13 DISCUSSION:

1. In what ways does the story of Naaman in 2 Kings 5:9-14 illustrate the consequences of pride and the benefits of humble submission?
2. How can we practically ensure that God's Word remains the final authority in our lives, especially in challenging situations?
3. Reflecting on Jesus' prayer in Luke 22:42-43, how can we better align our desires with the leading of the Holy Spirit?
4. Why is it often challenging for Christians to submit to God's people, and how can we cultivate a more submissive and humble attitude toward others in our church community?
5. How do you personally handle situations where you are asked to do something you feel is beneath you, and what steps can you take to respond more like Naaman after he humbled himself?

REFLECT ON WHAT THE HOLY SPIRIT SPOKE TO YOU IN THIS CHAPTER:

Chapter 14

The Suffering of Persecution

But may the God of all grace, who called us to His eternal glory by Christ Jesus, after you have suffered a while, perfect, establish, strengthen, and settle you.

1 Peter 5:10

When we talk about suffering, the end result should be us being perfected, established, strengthened, and settled by the grace of God. If that were truly the case in most churches, then the topic of suffering would be preached more often than it currently is. Suffering has been taught wrong for many years, and people have an unhealthy relationship with it. The response of most of the church when they hear about suffering is dread.

In my time as a pastor, I've noticed that there are different groups of people who understand suffering completely differently from each other. There are us, those who are learning what the Bible actually says about it, and then there are those who relate suffering to anything that hurts or causes discomfort. I just call these two groups Christians and Carnal Christians.

Christians believe in God's Word and have a clear understanding of God's promises in our lives that concern our healing, deliverance, prosperity, well-being, relationships, families, and everything in between. But then the Carnal Christians think that whatever hurts in their life, whether it's a sickness, oppression, poverty, marital issues, prodigal children, and everything in between, it must be God's will for them to suffer through to be a better person in the long run. They are adding things to the Bible that shouldn't be added.

And then you'll have another group of Christians that will completely disregard the suffering of any kind. These Christians give faith a bad name because they don't acknowledge the Word of God concerning suffering, and they think they are just too blessed and too favored to ever suffer in this life. That is wrong, too. What they are doing is performing a Scripurectomy. They cut out parts of the Bible that they don't like or agree with. True suffering is required for us to be perfected, strengthened, established, and settled. But it definitely is not related to anything and everything that hurts in our lives. Those things might make you suffer, but you're suffering something you don't have to suffer from with those things.

SUFFER LIKE JESUS

> *For to you it has been granted on behalf of Christ, not only to believe in Him, but also to suffer for His sake.*
>
> Philippians 1:29

To understand this, we need to pay close attention to the words in this scripture. The Bible has zero idle words in it. I believe that every single word is inspired by God to be included in it, including the periods and commas. Paul said that we've been granted to "suffer for His sake." In other words, if it is not for His sake, it's not for us to suffer.

We've already discussed what suffering is not, and then we ventured into one area of suffering that every believer is subject to, which is the suffering of submission. But there are still believers out there who will always relate suffering to our health, wealth, and prosperity. That message usually says that we have to be sick, we have to be poor, and we have to go through hardship. But that is not the Gospel. In fact, in the New Testament, you will not find suffering to be related to health, wealth, or prosperity anywhere. You will not find Paul writing in his letters, "I am so poor, but I am learning my lesson. Praise God." People have made assumptions and probabilities, but those are just opinions, and just like noses, everyone has them, and they always have a few holes in them. Those people are called Poverty Preachers, and they usually *hate* any message that deals with health, wealth, and prosperity.

> *Beloved, do not think it strange concerning the fiery trial which is to try you, as though some strange thing happened to you; but rejoice to the extent that you partake of Christ's sufferings, that when His glory is revealed, you may also be glad with exceeding joy. If you are reproached for the name of Christ, blessed are you, for the Spirit of glory and of God rests upon you. On their part He is blasphemed, but on your part He is glorified...*
>
> **1 Peter 4:12-14**

Peter liked to talk about suffering in his writings, but you always find a theme in how he relates our suffering. It's always according to the will of God, and it never deals with health, wealth, or prosperity. Notice Peter tells us not to think that these fiery trials (that come from the devil and not God) are some strange things happening to us. In other words, don't freak out or be surprised when the fiery trial comes because it should be expected! Instead, we should be able to rejoice. But then he goes on to say something very profound, and you need to understand this. He says, "*But rejoice to the extent that you partake of Christ's sufferings*" (1 Peter 4:13).

Think about this for a moment. What did Jesus Christ suffer from when He was on the earth? Was Jesus ever sick? The answer to that is no. Jesus never suffered from allergies or the common cold. He was in perfect health.

Was Jesus ever poor? Most people don't know this answer and assume that He was, but the reality is that Jesus was not poor. He may not have been a millionaire by today's standards, but He was not poor. Every single need was met, and He was able to bless people out of the abundance of His ministry. Not to mention, Jesus had a treasurer in charge of the finances. I don't know about you, but I don't have a treasure in my personal finances. You don't really need a treasurer when you don't have any money.

Jesus never suffered from allergies or the common cold. He was in perfect health.

People like to quote verses like Matthew 8:20 that say, "Foxes have holes and birds of the air have nests, but the Son of Man has nowhere to lay His head" and relate that to His poverty. This doesn't mean that He was so poor that He couldn't afford a pillow. What it means is that He was a traveling minister. There was no home for Him and the disciples. It says in 2 Corinthians 8:9 that Jesus literally became poor so that through His poverty, we could become rich. Relative to His riches in Heaven, where the streets are paved with gold, He became poor for us. You can't become poor unless you're rich.

What did Jesus actually suffer from? If we are to rejoice knowing that we partaking of the same sufferings of Jesus, we need to find out what Jesus suffered from. If He didn't suffer from sickness or poverty or anything else that many Christians are wrongfully suffering from today, then what is left?

> *If you are* ***reproached*** *for the name of Christ, blessed are you, for the Spirit of glory and of God rests upon you. On their part He is blasphemed, but on your part He is glorified…Therefore let those who suffer according to the will of God commit their souls to Him in doing good, as to a faithful Creator.*
>
> **1 Peter 4:14 & 19**

The same sufferings that Jesus partook in are the reproaches for the name of Jesus. The reproach of people not liking what we have to say about Jesus and the Word of God is the suffering we will face. So evidently, there is suffering that is according to the will of God, which means that there is also suffering that is *not* according to God's will. What we have to do as believers is be quick to identify: is this something I'm supposed to be resisting? If there is a suffering according to God's will and one that is not, we have to be quick to identify which one to resist. If we don't, we will submit to the wrong type of suffering.

When sickness comes, and you have no idea if it's from God or not, and you are quick to submit to it and think it's God trying to teach you a lesson, that is how you suffer more and longer than you need to. When financial burdens come knocking and trying to destroy your life, you have to know whether or not it is something to resist or submit to. Sadly, most Christians end up submitting to these things because they do not know.

As you know from the last chapter, Jesus has not redeemed us from suffering from submission. Submitting ourselves under God's will for our lives is extremely important if we want to experience the fullness of life that God has in store for us.

We also need to understand that Jesus hasn't redeemed us from resisting the devil. Resisting the devil is our main job. We have to resist the devil when he tries to attack us. If we don't, he will eat our lunch and pop the bag. The devil is our adversary, yet many in the body of Christ make the devil seem non-existent and blame everything on God's sovereignty. They are making the devil's job really easy.

Pretending that the devil doesn't exist doesn't make him any less of a threat. You need to understand that he is a zero with the rim knocked off, but if you don't realize that he is very good at deceiving Christians into handing over their rights and authority in Christ, you will lose every time. The devil is always against us and always our enemy. We have a God who loves us and wants the best for us and an enemy who hates us and is trying to steal, kill, and destroy. Where do you think sickness and hardship come from?

PRESSURE TO FALL AWAY

And lastly, Jesus hasn't redeemed us from persecution or reproaches. But do you know what He did do? He went through it, dealt with it, and then showed us how to do the same thing. If you haven't experienced persecution in your life, it's coming. It is better to prepare yourself now before the flood comes.

> *These likewise are the ones sown on stony ground who, when they hear the word, immediately receive it with gladness; and they have no root in themselves, and so endure only for a time. Afterward, when tribulation or persecution arises for the word's sake, immediately they stumble.*
>
> **Mark 4:16-17**

Yes, we really are talking about this parable again because it's that important. The King James Version substitutes the word *stumble* for *offended*. The Greek translates this word to where we get the word *scandal*. Scandals usually cause someone to stop trusting in the person involved in the scandal. If the devil can trip you up and make you untrustworthy, he will. But there is another translation to the word offended, which means "to cause to fall away or a falling out." Have you known someone for a really long time, and certain events took place between your friendships that caused a fallout? You went down one road, and they went down another road. There was a separation that took place–a scattering.

If you do some studying, you'll find out that the words tribulation and persecution are often describing the same thing. When tribulation comes or when persecution comes, there is pressure attached to it. When you hear someone preaching about the end times, often you'll hear them mention The Great Tribulation. The Great Tribulation is the period of time when the anti-Christ will be ruling, and believers will be raptured with Jesus. During this time, the anti-Christ isn't going to be afflicting people with sickness and diseases; he doesn't have the power to do that. But what he will be doing is putting pressure on people. This period of *tribulation* is going to be a period of great pressure.

If the devil can trip you up and make you untrustworthy, he will.

We need to stop using these words without intentionality because they contain valuable truths. Whenever you read about tribulation or persecution, look further, and you'll find pressure attached to both. There are many stories in the New Testament that have this type of pressure in them.

> *Now Saul was consenting to [Stephen's] death. At that time a great persecution arose against the church which was at Jerusalem; and they were all scattered throughout the regions of Judea and Samaria, except the apostles.*
>
> **Acts 8:1, brackets added**

This was the Apostle Paul before his conversion to Christianity. He was out there persecuting the church in Jerusalem religiously, and in this instance, he was sentencing this man, Stephen, to death by being stoned. He was out on a mission to get the known world rid of Christians.

SCATTERED

This church in Jerusalem started on the day of Pentecost. The disciples were in an upper room filled with 120 people in it. There, the Holy Spirit fell upon everyone in the room, and the power of God was released. This was the fulfillment of the promise that Jesus had made to them many times prior.

Because of this amazing encounter with the Holy Spirit, Peter stepped out of the room and started preaching to everyone and anyone who would listen to him. The very same day that the first church was created, it grew into a mega church. It started with 120 people, then grew to over 3,000 people, and within a few months, this church grew to over 100,000 people scattered throughout Jerusalem.

But then this event happened, and Paul started persecuting the church. This would cause the church to scatter and disperse from each other. The only ones to remain together were the Apostles. Everyone else scattered throughout Judea and Samaria. When persecution came, they scattered. This is a perfect example of what the devil meant for evil, God turned it around for good. God wasn't the one who persecuted the church. The devil did that.

But what the devil didn't know was that the church would then use that to its advantage and start planting churches throughout the known regions. It fueled their fire! This church was unstoppable. The danger in persecution is that it can cause you to disconnect from what's bringing you life. The devil will try to separate you from your life source if you let him, but if you can remain planted in the body of Christ, you will thrive under any condition.

> *Then Jesus said to them, All of you will be made to stumble because of Me this night, for it is written: I will strike the Shepherd, And the sheep of the flock will be scattered.*
>
> Matthew 26:31

Do you see the tactic of persecution and what it does to the church? It causes people to withdraw from each other and disassociate with that group of people because of pressure. The enemy is trying to put pressure on you and your pastors every single day to get you away from what is giving you life. This is what Jesus warned His disciples about before He was crucified. He told them that they would all be scattered because He would be persecuted.

The word "scattered" here is the same exact word "offended" in Mark chapter 4. Because of the amount of persecution that was on Jesus, the result was that His disciples all left Him. And the persecution that was on the church in Jerusalem caused everyone to leave each other and scatter.

Satan can put so much heat on one individual that it can cause fear in the people around him, and they disconnect and scatter. I know of a great minister that many people do not like simply because he is bold and preaches the Word of God how it is. They have labeled him a health, wealth, and prosperity preacher and distance themselves from him and anyone else who follows his ministry.

I've witnessed this firsthand. One time, I was interviewing for a pastoral job at a church in my hometown. The interview was being held by the lead pastor at the time and some of their board members. We were discussing qualifications and the scope of the job that I would be taking on. It was a great interview. It was so great that I was sure I had sealed the deal. But then they asked me about some of my favorite books that I've read.

I was being honest with them and told them, "I actually don't read too many books. I mainly just read the Bible. But if I do read anything, it's usually a book from Andrew Wommack." The room got quiet, and no one really said anything for a few seconds, which felt like minutes. After a few more points were discussed, the interview ended, and I still felt great about my odds of getting the position.

The next day, I received a phone call from the lead pastor himself. Stephanie was in the car next to me when I got the call, and I picked up the phone with pure confidence.

"Hey, Matthew! Hope you're doing well. We were just going over the interview yesterday and evaluating whether or not you're a good fit for this position. We loved everything you said and everything about you. We think you'd be great for this position...but..."

And there it was.

He continued to say, "There's just this one thing. This guy that you mentioned. We can't have that. In fact, I believe that your theology is actually detrimental and hogwash if you ask me."

In essence, he told me that if I didn't renounce him and his teachings, I couldn't be on their staff. I didn't get the job in case you were wondering. Not only was he upset about the guy that I mentioned, but he started insulting me when I didn't do anything to him. He was offended. He started to scatter away from me all because of what I believe.

This is exactly what Jesus had experienced with His own disciples. If it happened to Jesus, it's going to happen to us, too, in some fashion. In fact, after Jesus had said these things to them about the sheep scattering because of Him, it says,

> *Peter answered and said to Him, Even if all are made to stumble because of You, I will never be made to stumble. Jesus said to him, Assuredly, I say to you that this night, before the rooster crows, you will deny Me three times. Peter said to Him, Even if I have to die with You, I will not deny You! And so said all the disciples.*
>
> **Matthew 26:33-35**

Peter, oh Peter. So full of self-confidence but has no discernment whatsoever. Kind of like the Israelites right before God gave them the first commandments. Before God had given them any commands to follow, the Israelites said, "Whatever you tell us to do, we can do it" (Exodus 19:8), and within days, they broke the first commandment.

Peter wasn't the only one to make this type of commitment. It says that all of the disciples said the same thing! Yet they all ended up falling away to some degree. It's recorded that Peter ended up following Jesus during His trials, but it specifically mentions Peter following from a distance (Matthew 26:58). And when the pressure came, and people started to notice Peter as Jesus' disciple, he got further and further from Jesus. There is a caution we have to be mindful of that we don't fall into pride like Peter and the disciples when the pressure comes.

Persecution is coming in this life, and if it isn't coming, it's been here already. The church has been experiencing persecution since the times of Jesus. And if they persecuted Him and the ones who followed Him, they are going to persecute us, too.

CANCEL CULTURE

Many people dismiss persecution, especially those who are Western Christians. They like to believe that persecution only happens to those who are missionaries in third-world countries or churches in hiding in communist China. Those places are absolutely experiencing a type of persecution that we are privileged enough not to face. People are literally dying because they are preaching the Gospel, while the Western Church is getting offended because someone commented something mean on our social media post. Some things need to be put into perspective. Most Christians aren't being persecuted in America; they just have thin skin. They're babies. If you're offended by this, then it's time to develop some thick skin and toughen up, you baby. News flash–the world doesn't love Jesus! That's why Peter said, "Don't think it's strange when the fiery trials come" (1 Peter 4:12).

Although we don't face persecution like Paul, Jesus, or Stephen in the Bible, we face persecution in different ways. We need to understand that persecution is not limited to life-and-death outcomes. Right now, our society has adopted this idea called Cancel Culture, which says if you don't like what someone is saying, they are canceled.

Big corporations who have the media influence to cancel someone have been taking advantage of this. If our church publishes a livestream on a Sunday morning and we say something that someone doesn't like, that video can be taken down!

Persecution is already here, and pressure is here, but the question is, what will you do when the pressure is in your life? When I think about pressure, I like to think about submarines. When a submarine dives under the water, it needs to be pressurized to the same pressure of the atmosphere above the water. The deeper that a submarine dives, the more intense pressure it will experience from the water. In order for it to keep from collapsing, it is by pushing pressure back out towards the water.

You have the Holy Spirit on the inside of you, strengthening you from the inside out.

When life starts to put pressure on you for what you believe or who you are associated with, are you going to collapse or are you going to push back? Now, I don't mean to push back by cussing people out like Peter did when he was pressured. There is no cussing in Jesus' name. But you have the Holy Spirit on the inside of you, strengthening you from the inside out.

Satan is trying to shame people to the point where you begin to disconnect from your faith. He wants you to stop sharing what God has done in your life. One of the areas I find the most resistance in is the area of healing. Whenever I share something about healing, without a doubt, I will have people come against me, saying, "My dad died of this sickness. How can you say God wants us healed?" That is the enemy trying to keep you from sharing the truth.

In 1 Timothy, the Apostle Paul was writing letters to this new young pastor, Timothy. Timothy's church is thriving. He's seeing new salvations and healings, and their church is growing exponentially like the church of Acts. Between 1st and 2nd Timothy, major persecution in the church started to develop. It first starts off as religious persecution, but then it develops into political persecution. In 2 Timothy, we see Paul writing letters to Timothy from prison because of this political persecution. Emporer Nero was the man in charge of Rome, and this is a point in the Roman Empire where Rome was at one of its strongest points in history.

THE ABANDONED APOSTLE

Empower Nero was crazy in the head and imprisoned Paul for false accusations of burning down Rome. While in prison, Paul writes to Timothy, telling him to continue being strong in the faith because God has given him a spirit of love, power, and a sound mind (2 Timothy 1:7). This was a time of major persecution in the church. Yet, Paul encourages Timothy not to back down. Not to give in. He then continues to encourage Timothy with the power of the Gospel of Jesus and says,

> *To which I was appointed a preacher, an apostle, and a teacher of the Gentiles. For this reason I also suffer these things; nevertheless I am not ashamed, for I know whom I have believed and am persuaded that He is able to keep what I have committed to Him until that Day.*
>
> **2 Timothy 1:11-12**

Paul was saying that he was appointed a preacher of the Gospel, and "for this reason" or because of being a preacher of the Gospel, he suffered. The entire subject of this scripture is persecution. Paul encourages Timothy not to back down, not to draw back, but to push forward. Because of the Word of God, persecution will come (Mark 4:17).

It would have an entirely different meaning if Paul had stated that he was suffering a sickness or ailment or disease, but that is not what he said. He suffered from persecution. The sad result of Paul's life was that because of the immense pressure that he faced, everyone who was once with him in the ministry left him (2 Timothy 1:15). The Apostle Paul, who turned the known world upside down with the revelation of grace, had everyone leave him because of persecution. If Jesus dealt with it, if Paul dealt with it, you can deal with it too.

One thing I've learned really quickly in the church is that people will do two things the best. People will come, and people will go. But what I've come to find out is that you can't let your head get too big when they come, and you can't let your heart get broken when they go. The number of people who have come and gone to our church is crazy, but I choose not to let it affect my passion.

I want to encourage you regarding persecution. In the moment, it might seem like the end of the world. You might not be able to see the other side of what you're facing, but God always makes a way.

> *But you have carefully followed my doctrine, manner of life, purpose, faith, longsuffering, love, perseverance, persecutions, afflictions, which happened to me at Antioch, at Iconium, at Lystra—what persecutions I endured. And out of them all the Lord delivered me. Yes, and all who desire to live godly in Christ Jesus will suffer persecution.*
>
> **2 Timothy 3:10-12**

Paul didn't let the persecution stop him from doing his ministry. He continued to be a role model for young Timothy to follow, and evidently, Timothy succeeded. Paul was able to get through the persecution and pressure because the Lord delivered him out of them all. It doesn't matter what you are facing; God can get you out of it. It doesn't matter the pushback you receive from people; God can get you out of it. If that doesn't light your fire, your wood is wet! In the last chaper of Paul's letter to Timothy, he expressed that even more people have left him, and only Luke was left. Everyone abandoned the great Apostle Paul. But do you know what got him through it?

> *At my first defense no one stood with me, but all forsook me. May it not be charged against them.* ***But the Lord stood with me and strengthened me****, so that the message might be preached fully through me, and that all the Gentiles might hear. Also I was delivered out of the mouth of the lion. And the Lord will deliver me from every evil work and preserve me for His heavenly kingdom. To Him be glory forever and ever. Amen!*
>
> **2 Timothy 4:16-18**

Wow. What a way to end. Regardless of his circumstances, regardless of the fact that literally everyone left him and abandoned him, he chose to acknowledge the truth that God never left him. The suffering of persecution was able to perfect, strengthen, establish, and settle Paul to finish his race. The same God who sustained Paul in his ministry is the same God who will sustain you when the pressure intensifies. Our call in life to suffer according to the will of God is the suffering of persecution, but we can press on if we focus on Jesus. We can get through the bad things people say about us if we stay mindful of the truth that sets us free.

CHAPTER 14 DISCUSSION:

1. How do "Christians" and "Carnal Christians" differ in their understanding of suffering?
2. What distinguishes suffering for Christ from suffering due to personal issues?
3. How is suffering from submission different from other forms of suffering?
4. What insights does Philippians 1:29 offer on suffering for Christ?
5. In what ways can persecution affect a believer's faith and community relationships?
6. What role does the devil play in suffering, and how can understanding this benefit believers?

REFLECT ON WHAT THE HOLY SPIRIT SPOKE TO YOU IN THIS CHAPTER:

Prayer To Receive Jesus

Making Jesus your personal Lord and Savior is the best decision you could ever make. The Bible says all the angels in heaven celebrate whenever one person is added to the Kingdom of God (Luke 15:10).

God promises *"that if you confess with your mouth the Lord Jesus and believe in your heart that God has raised Him from the dead, you will be saved. For with the heart one believes unto righteousness, and with the mouth confession is made unto salvation"* (Romans 10:9-10) and, *"For whoever calls on the name of the Lord shall be saved"* (Romans 10:13).

You are a *whoever*! These scriptures guarantee if you believe and confess, you will be saved. It is the best guarantee in the universe!

Ephesians tells us that we are saved by God's grace through our faith in His promises. God's grace was Jesus dying on the cross for you to have a relationship with God. The faith part is your response to God's grace. By accepting Jesus and believing, you have responded by faith!

I hope you pray the following prayer out loud. Don't worry about who hears you or what people think. This is your moment to change your life forever.

Pray, "Dear Jesus, thank you for dying on the cross for my sins. I confess that you are my personal Lord and Savior. I believe that you died on the cross and rose from the dead. Through faith, I accept, and I receive your gift of salvation. I am no longer a sinner, but I am the righteousness of God through You. Thank you for saving my life. Amen."

Congratulations, my friend! You have now become a part of God's family. There are so many promises and blessings coming your way. By putting faith in God's Word, you are instantly a brand new creation with a brand new spirit. I want to give you a free gift.

Visit **matthewochoa.com** for a free book describing what just happened on the inside of you. I am so proud of you.

Prayer To Receive The Holy Spirit

God promises the gift of the Holy Spirit to all who will believe. Listen to the words of Jesus:

> *For everyone who asks receives, and he who seeks finds, and to him who knocks it will be opened. If a son asks for bread from any father among you, will he give him a stone? Or if he asks for a fish, will he give him a serpent instead of a fish? Or if he asks for an egg, will he offer him a scorpion? If you then, being evil, know how to give good gifts to your children, how much more will your heavenly Father give the Holy Spirit to those who ask Him!*
>
> **Luke 11:10-13**

Because you are now God's child, the first gift (besides salvation) that God wants you to have is the gift of the Holy Spirit. This gift harnesses the supernatural power that you need to be victorious in the Christian life. The same way you asked, believed, and received salvation is the same way you can ask, believe, and receive the gift of the Holy Spirit.

Pray this out loud: "Father, I can do nothing by myself. I need Your power to be victorious in life. I ask You to fill me with the Holy Spirit. Through faith, I accept and receive this gift right now. Thank you for baptizing me in the Spirit. Holy Spirit, You are welcome to dwell in my life to teach me and guide me in all areas of my life."

You have now been filled with the supernatural power of God!

After you receive the Holy Spirit, you might speak in an unknown tongue, which is perfectly alright (1 Corinthians 14:14). If you speak in tongues, you'll release God's supernatural power into your life by faith. This isn't a one-time deal; you can speak in tongues whenever you want.

On the other hand, don't worry if you don't experience changes right away. What matters is if you believe in your heart that you have received the Holy Spirit. God's Word promises you will receive the Spirit whether you feel it or not, and God never goes back on His Word. Believe you have received it!

If you receive Jesus as your Savior and become filled with the Holy Spirit, I would love to hear from you. I would be honored to congratulate you and help you get started with your new faith walk with Jesus. Praise God! You are a new person, a new creation! (2 Corinthians 5:17). Welcome to your new life!

About the Author

Matthew Ochoa, born and raised in Visalia, California, embraced a life of faith from an early age. His spiritual journey began in the backseat of his parents' SUV, where he committed to following Jesus. At nineteen, Matthew experienced a powerful transformation when he was baptized in the Holy Spirit at a young adult camp.

That same year, he began a relationship with Stephanie, who would become his wife and partner in ministry. They married two years later, entering into a covenant with God that has profoundly shaped their lives and ministry together.

After high school, Matthew attended a leadership school, where he felt God's call to start Matthew Ochoa Ministries. This platform allows Matthew and Stephanie to share the transformative message of God's unconditional love, grace, and power. In 2021, they founded Deep Rooted Church, a thriving community where lives are being transformed each week. As the lead pastor, Matthew reaches a global audience through Sunday services, podcasts, social media, and his international broadcast, Rooted & Grounded.

Matthew and Stephanie reside in Visalia, California, where they continue to pastor Deep Rooted Church. They are blessed with one son, born in February 2023, and eagerly await the birth of their second child in December 2024.

Matthew is passionate about making his teachings accessible to all, offering them for free to those who cannot afford them. His dedication to preaching God's Word without compromise aims to help everyone experience the abundant life Jesus promised.

To learn more about Pastor Matthew and his ministry, please visit **matthewochoa.com**.

CONTACT INFORMATION

Matthew Ochoa Ministries
PO BOX 254
Visalia, CA 93279

Email: info@matthewochoa.com
Phone: 559-212-4827

www.matthewochoa.com

JOIN US FOR CHURCH!

Sundays at 10AM
1001 W Noble Ave,
Visalia, CA 93277

www.deeprooted.church

Milton Keynes UK
Ingram Content Group UK Ltd.
UKHW052359201024
449919UK00016B/158